PEARSON LANGUAGE CENTRAL

PEARSON

Upper Saddle River, New Jersey • Boston, Massachusetts
Chandler, Arizona • Glenview, Illinois

Pearson Language Central Contributing Authors

The following authors guided the direction and philosophy
of English Language Learner instruction and support in
Pearson *Literature.* Their scholarship and advice informed
the development of *Language Central.*

Grant Wiggins

Maria V. Balderrama

Arnetha F. Ball

Danling Fu

Sharroky Hollie

Julie Maravilla

ISBN-13: 978-0-13-370442-6
ISBN-10:   0-13-370442-4

6 7 8 9 10   V092   15 14 13

Grade 10 Contents

Unit 1 Is there a difference between reality and truth? 1

Contents

Grade 10 Contents

Unit 2 Can progress be made without conflict?

iv

Grade 10 Contents

Unit 5 — To what extent does experience determine what we perceive?

Grade 10 Contents

How to Use This Book

This book will help you make connections to what you are learning in your English Language Arts class. You will **learn** new vocabulary words, **read** new nonfiction passages, and **practice** language, comprehension, and writing.

Learn New Vocabulary

Start each lesson with new vocabulary words. Each word has a definition for you to understand. These words connect to the **Big Question** and topics you are studying in your English Language Arts class.

Read a Passage

You will read several nonfiction passages. Each passage has the new vocabulary words you have learned. The passages are also connected to the main lesson topic.

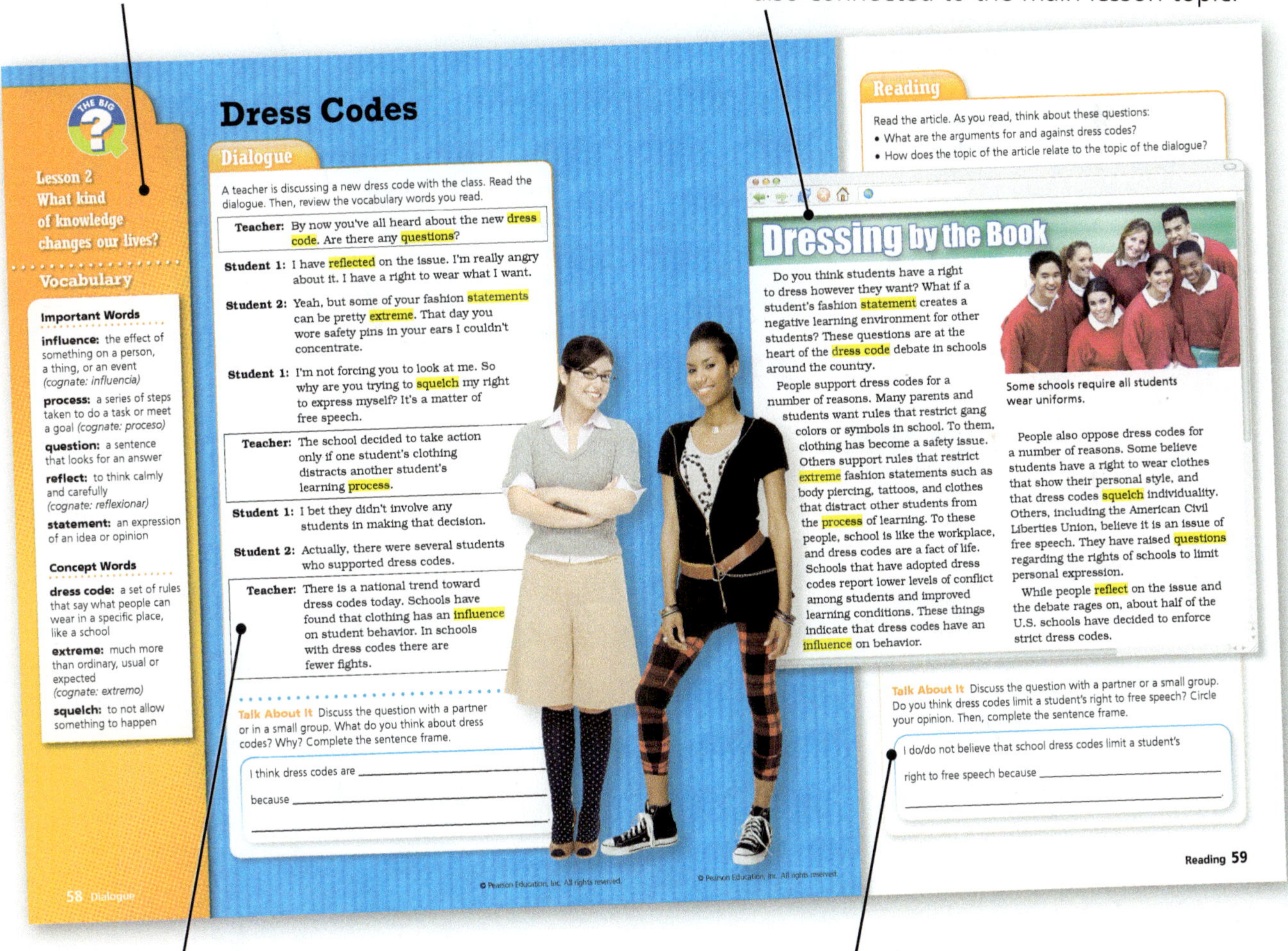

Read a Dialogue

Practice your new **vocabulary** with dialogues. Each lesson will have a dialogue that goes with the lesson topic.

Respond to the Passage

After you read, answer questions about the passage. Then, **practice English** by talking about your answers with your classmates.

How to Use This Book

Learn Language and Comprehension

As you become a better reader and thinker, you will need to understand **academic language**—the words of reading and thinking. Each lesson has a page where you can practice this language.

Talk About It

You can practice **discussing** with your classmates what you have learned and how it will make you a better reader and thinker.

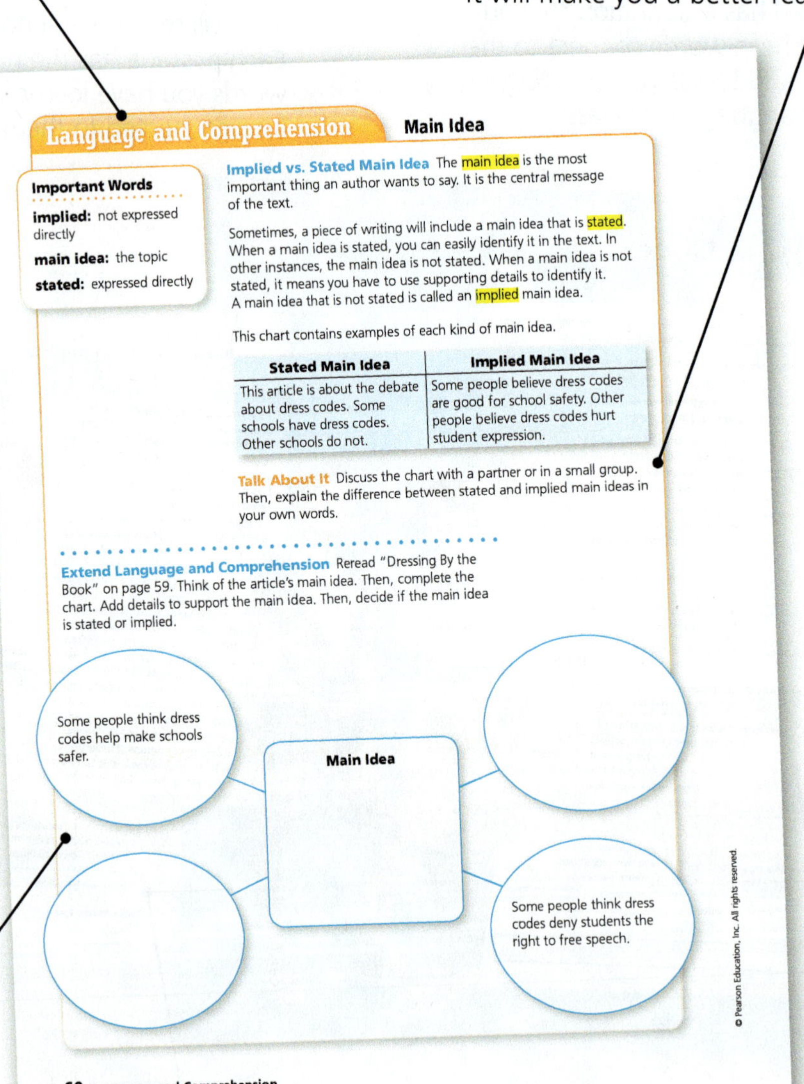

Practice Comprehension

Each lesson will include **charts** and **graphic organizers** to help you to understand what you are reading. They will also help you to record important information.

G2

Connect to Writing

You will write about what you have learned. To help you improve your writing in English, you will write **sentences,** make **outlines,** and write **paragraphs.**

Connect to Writing

Main Idea Paragraph Think of all you have learned in this lesson. What new words did you use? How did you learn to distinguish between implied and stated main ideas? How did you find the main idea? Talk with a partner about what you learned.

Now, write your own paragraph. Use the topic of school dress codes. Think of your main idea and supporting details. On a separate sheet of paper, make sure to include

• a clear main idea.

• at least three supporting details.

If you need help, use the sentence frames.

Dress codes are ______________________________

______________________________.

For example, ______________________________

______________________________.

This has reduced ______________________________

______________________________.

As a result, ______________________________

______________________________.

Writing Tips
Don't forget to

1. think of why you are including details.

2. make sure the details support the main idea.

3. use effective transitions.

Extension Activity   Writing

Write a Descriptive Essay On a separate sheet of paper or on a computer, describe your ideal school uniform. Describe what it would look like and how it would appeal to everyone in the school. Explain why you made the choices you did.

Tips for Your Essay

• Remember that this is not just *your* uniform, and that everyone in the school will be wearing something similar.

• Use vivid and expressive language.

• Be reasonable. Be aware of your school's current dress guidelines.

• Use the Writing Process Handbook at the end of this book. This will help you with prewriting, drafting, and revising. If you are writing on a computer, follow the directions for your word-processing program.

Connect to Writing **61**

Extension Activities

At the end of each lesson, you will explore the lesson topic through **Listening and Speaking, Research,** or **Writing.** This will help you to think about the Big Question.

G3

An Introduction to Literary Terms

This year in your Reading and Language Arts class, you will be reading many types of literature. These pages contain definitions of the different kinds of literature you will read with your teacher and classmates. You can use these pages during your school year if you have questions about the kinds of literature you are reading.

There are two categories of literature: fiction and nonfiction.

Fiction

Fiction is writing that is imaginative. The main purpose of fiction to is entertain readers. In fiction, the author creates events and characters. Here are some examples of fiction:

Short Stories

Novels

Myths and Legends

Drama

Nonfiction

Nonfiction is writing about real people and events. The main purpose of nonfiction is to inform readers. In this *Language Central* book, you will be reading nonfiction. You will also read nonfiction in your Reading and Language Arts class. Here are some examples of nonfiction:

Essays

Speeches

Autobiographies

Biographies

Talk About It Discuss these questions with a partner or in a small group. What kind of writing do you like to read? Do you like to read fiction? Do you like to read nonfiction? What do you like better, fiction or nonfiction? Create a list based on your discussion.

I like to read ___________________ because ___________________

____.

I think ___________________ is better than ___________________

because ____.

Different Types of Fiction

Here are some definitions for different kinds of fiction.

Type of Fiction	Examples from Literature
short story a brief work of prose fiction which includes plot, setting, characters, point of view and theme	"The Monkey's Paw" W.W. Jacobs
novel fiction which is book-length and has more plot and character details than a short story	*Don Quixote* Miguel de Cervantes
myth an important story, often part of a culture's religion or history, which explains how the world came to be or why natural events happen	"Cupid and Psyche" Lucius Apuleius, retold by Sally Benson
drama a story told through the words and actions of characters, written to be performed as well as read; a play	*A Problem* Anton Chekhov

Talk About It Discuss the chart with a partner or in a small group. Why do you think these examples are good examples of fiction? What is your favorite type of fiction? Create your own chart based on your discussion.

I think these are good examples of fiction because ___________________

____.

My favorite type of fiction is ___________________ because _________

____.

Different Types of Nonfiction

Here are some definitions for different types of nonfiction.

Type of Nonfiction	Examples from Literature
essay a written work which shows the writer's opinions on some basic or current issue	"The Sun Parlor" Dorothy West
speech a type of essay which can be read aloud and contains language which can inform, entertain, or persuade readers	"Keep Memory Alive" Elie Wiesel
autobiography a person's life story, written by that person	*Swimming to Antarctica* Lynne Cox
biography a person's life story, written by someone else	"Marian Anderson, Famous Concert Singer" Langston Hughes

Talk About It Discuss the chart with a partner or in a small group. Why do you think these examples are good examples of nonfiction? What is your favorite type of nonfiction? Create a list of historical speeches with your partner or group, and write it on a separate sheet of paper. Choose one speech and discuss what features make it memorable.

I think these are good examples of nonfiction because ______________________

____ .

My favorite type of nonfiction is ____

because ____

____ .

Different Types of Poetry

Poetry is a type of literature that usually has rhythm. A poem can use words to create powerful or beautiful images. Some poems have sound patterns, such as rhyme. Most songs are types of poetry set to music.

As you read different types of literature, you will find that poetry, in particular, comes in a variety of different forms. You will be required to identify these forms.

from "My City"
James Weldon Johnson

When I come down to sleep death's endless night,
The threshold of the unknown dark to cross,
What to me then will be the keenest loss,
When this bright world blurs on my fading sight?
5 Will it be that no more I shall see the trees
Or smell the flowers or hear the singing birds
Or watch the flashing streams or patient herds?

Type of Poetry	Examples from Your Reading Class
epic a long narrative poem which tells a story, often dealing with adventure, tragedy, or romance	*Morte d'Arthur* Alfred, Lord Tennyson
lyric a brief poem, often with musical qualities, in which the author expresses the feelings of a single speaker, creating a single effect on the reader	"The Guitar" Federico García Lorca
dramatic verse in which the writer tells a story using a character's own thoughts or statements	"Danny Deever" Rudyard Kipling
sonnet a poem with fourteen lines which has a formal tone and follows a specific rhyme pattern	"Sonnet 18" William Shakespeare

Talk About It Work with a partner or in a small group. Choose a poem, a piece of fiction, and a piece of nonfiction all about the same topic. Compare and contrast the different ways the topic is written about. Which one do you like best? Why? Complete the sentence frame.

I like the ____

best because ____

____

____.

Is there a difference between reality and truth?

In this unit, I will read:

In this unit, I will:

- learn new vocabulary words.
- read about different topics.
- use my background knowledge.
- use question words.
- use cause and effect words.
- visualize details.
- learn about how to make predictions.
- learn about cause and effect.
- write a background knowledge paragraph.
- write a problem and solution essay.
- write a research report.
- write a poem.

Is there a difference between reality and truth?

Connect to the Big Question

Answer these questions. Discuss your answers with your teacher and classmates.

How can you tell what is reality? How can you tell what is truth?

Extend the Big Question

Read each sentence frame. Write your opinions in each blank.

I think reality is _______________

____

____

____

____

____

_______________________.

I think truth is _______________

____

____

____

____

____

_______________________.

Discuss your opinions with your teacher and classmates.

Big Question Words

Use your definitions from page 1 of the *Review and Assess* book.

comprehend
(cognate: *comprender*)

concrete
(cognate: *concreto*)

confirm
(cognate: *confirmar*)

context
(cognate: *contexto*)

differentiate
(cognate: *diferenciar*)

discern
(cognate: *discernir*)

evaluate
(cognate: *evaluar*)

evidence
(cognate: *evidencia*)

improbable
(cognate: *improbable*)

objective
(cognate: *objetivo*)

perception
(cognate: *percepción*)

reality
(cognate: *realidad*)

subjective
(cognate: *subjetivo*)

uncertainty
(cognate: *incertidumbre*)

verify
(cognate: *verificar*)

Vocabulary Workshop

Answer the Questions Read each question. Choose a word from the Big Question Words to answer each question. Write your answer on the line.

1. What would you find at a crime scene?

   ____

2. What word means "based on feelings and opinions"?

   ____

3. What word means the same as "unlikely"?

   ____

4. What word means almost the same as "to check to make sure"? _______________________________

5. What word means "understanding"?

   ____

Use Context Fill in the lines with Big Question Words.

I awoke to a loud bang! My bedroom was so dark, my sense of _______________________ was nonexistent. I could not _______________________ between the door and the walls. My first thought was that someone had burst into my room, and I was a little scared. I reminded myself to _______________________ the situation and look for _______________________ evidence before making conclusions. Finally, I was able to _______________________ the light switch on the wall. I flicked on the light, and when I saw my tennis trophy on the floor, I knew this mystery was solved!

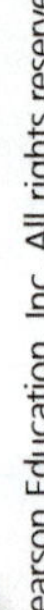

Word Roots A word's root can give you clues about that word's meaning.

A root is the basic part of a word. It usually contains a word's basic meaning. Prefixes and suffixes can be added to a root to change its meaning.

For example, the word *verify* contains the Latin root *ver*, meaning "truth." Therefore, *verify* means to check the truth of something.

The police asked around to *verify* the suspect's story.

The police asked around to *check the truth* of the suspect's story.

Find the Root Circle the root in each of the following words. Write each word's definition. If you need help, use a dictionary.

plantation _______________________ _______________________	portable _______________________ _______________________
proceed _______________________ _______________________	submarine _______________________ _______________________
dismal _______________________ _______________________	absent _______________________ _______________________

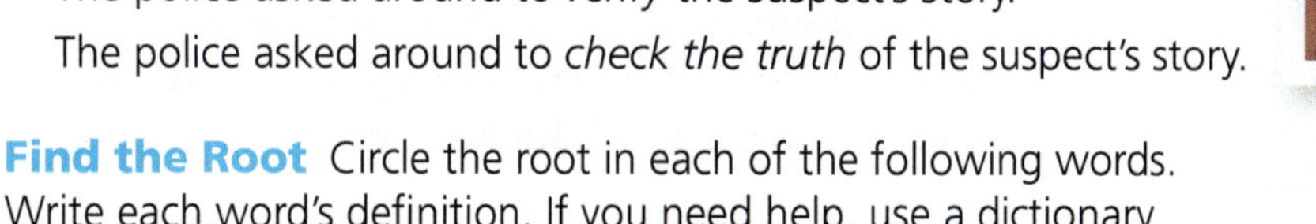

Word Origins Sometimes knowing a word's origin can help you understand unfamiliar words. Many words in English come from different places and languages.

For example, you can use a dictionary to look up the origin of the word *perception*. The word comes from the Latin word *percipere*, which means "be aware of." Also, if you know Spanish, this word is very similar to the Spanish word *percepción*.

Find the Origin Choose three Big Question Words from page 3. Then, use a dictionary to find the word's place of origin. Write the word and the word's origin in the chart below.

Word:	**Origin:**
Word:	**Origin:**
Word:	**Origin:**

Lesson 1
Is there a difference between reality and truth?

Vocabulary

Important Words

comprehend: to understand something *(cognate: comprender)*

improbable: when something can happen but is not likely to *(cognate: improbable)*

involve: to include or be part of something *(cognate: involucrar)*

subjective: based on feelings or opinions rather than facts *(cognate: sujetivo)*

verify: to check whether or not something is true *(cognate: verificar)*

Concept Words

luck: something that brings good or bad things to someone

unlucky: to have bad luck

winnings: something won, especially money

Luck

Dialogue

A parent and two teenagers are talking about winning the lottery. Read the dialogue. Then, discuss the vocabulary words you read.

Teen 1: Did you see the lottery winnings are worth $20 million this week? I wish I could win.

Parent: Can you comprehend how improbable the chances of winning the lottery are? You would have to have a lot of luck on your side to win.

Teen 2: I guess the word luck is subjective. For example, I think some lottery winners are unlucky. I think having that much money involves a lot of problems.

Teen 1: What kinds of problems?

Teen 2: Everyone would want some of your winnings. Plus, you would have to learn a lot about handling finances.

Teen 1: Those are problems I would risk having to win $20 million.

Parent: You don't actually get the whole $20 million. After taxes are taken out you only get a fraction of the actual winnings. So you would need to verify your actual income before spending.

Teen 2: What would you do with the money?

Teen 1: I'd get a giant house and new car for each of us. We could get new clothes and entertainment systems, and go on long vacations.

Teen 2: You would run out of money in a week. Then, you'd be back where you started.

Talk About It Discuss with a partner or in a group. What if you won the lottery? How would you spend the money? Complete the sentence frame.

I would ____
____
____.

Read the article. As you read, think about these questions:
- What is lucky about winning the lottery?
- What makes some winners unlucky?

What would you do if you won $16 million? Winning the lottery is so **improbable** that most winners feel they are full of **luck**. However, most people don't consider the negative effects of winning the lottery. One winner from Pennsylvania realized the effects when he said, "I was much happier when I was broke." How can winning the lottery be **unlucky**?

Soon after winning, the Pennsylvania man became **involved** in some business ventures to please his family, but he didn't **verify** their worth. Then, he bought an airplane and a huge house he could barely afford. He couldn't seem to **comprehend** the concept of money management. He had frequent arguments over finances with his wife and family, and he was sued by his landlady who bought him the lottery ticket. Soon, the man had no money.

Another lottery winner in New Jersey gave away most of her $5 million **winnings**. She lost the rest of the money because she had a gambling problem. She told one reporter, "I won the American dream, but I lost it, too."

Experts say that many lottery winners make some common mistakes. First, they give money away to family members, friends, and charities without making careful decisions. Next, they buy expensive luxuries without managing their expenses. Deciding whether or not these people were "lucky" or "unlucky" is very **subjective**.

It's not how much money you have, but what you do with it.

Talk About It Discuss with a partner or in a group. Do you think it is lucky or unlucky to win the lottery? Why? Use the sentence frame.

I think winning the lottery is _________________________________

because ____

____.

Important Words

background: a person's experience or knowledge

formulate: to create and to prepare
(cognate: formular)

predict: to figure out what might happen next
(cognate: predecir)

Background Knowledge Background knowledge is something that you already know about the text, the topic, or the author. Background knowledge can help you to understand what you are reading and to predict, or formulate, ideas about what might happen next.

Talk About It Discuss the questions with a partner or in a group. What background knowledge did you use in the "Unlucky Winners" article? How did it help you understand what you were reading?

Extend Language and Comprehension
Read the story. Then, use your background knowledge and story details to make a prediction in the chart below.

Before winning the lottery, Janice watched her spending closely and only bought the things she needed. But after she won $10 million, her friends didn't even recognize her. She spent her days shopping online for her favorite clothes and products. She bought a sports car that didn't fit her personality at all. She also looked into buying a yacht, even though she had never liked boats. The money was going very quickly.

Story Details: But after she won $10 million, her friends didn't even recognize her.

Background Knowledge: ____

____

Prediction:____

____

Connect to Writing

Background Knowledge Paragraph Think of all you have learned in this lesson. What new words did you use? How did you use background knowledge to make predictions?

On a separate sheet of paper, write a paragraph that answers the following questions:

- Why is background knowledge useful in predicting actions or events?
- What kind of background knowledge helps you predict how characters will act?

If you need help, use the sentence frames.

Background knowledge about ________________________________

____

helps you predict events by ________________________________

____.

Background knowledge about ________________________________

____.

helps you predict how characters will act because ______________

____.

Extension Activity   Writing

Write an Essay On separate paper or on a computer, write a problem-and-solution essay about people who win the lottery and then spend all their money. First, explain the unexpected problems that arise with the sudden gain of a huge amount of money. Then, think about the things you would do if you won the lottery, and propose your ideas as solutions.

Tips for Your Essay

- State the problem clearly.
- Propose a solution that is reasonable and practical.
- Use the Writing Process Handbook at the end of this book. This will help you with prewriting, drafting, and revising.
- If you are writing on a computer, follow the directions for your word-processing program.

Lesson 2
Is there a difference between reality and truth?

Vocabulary

Important Words

evidence: detail that shows that something is true (*cognate: evidencia*)

intent: a purpose

objective: based on facts rather than on opinions or feelings (*cognate: objetivo*)

perception: what you see or understand about things that happen around you (*cognate: percepción*)

reality: real things, facts, or events (*cognate: realidad*)

Concept Words

discrimination: treating people unfairly because they belong to a particular group (*cognate: discriminación*)

salary: the money you make for a job (*cognate: salario*)

wage gap: the difference between men's pay and women's pay

Gender and Wages

Dialogue

Two teens are talking about job discrimination. Read the dialogue. Then, discuss the vocabulary words you read.

Teen 1: What are you going to do your report on?

Teen 2: I'm going to talk about the wage gap, or pay difference between men and women. Women and men still don't make an equal salary for the same jobs.

Teen 1: I thought men and women were equal in the workplace since the 1960s. After all, women are lawyers, doctors, and business leaders.

Teen 2: That's a common perception many people have, but the reality is that women are paid less.

Teen 1: Really? I find it hard to believe that employers are guilty of that kind of discrimination.

Teen 2: An employer's intent may not be to discriminate, but they might still hold old-fashioned ideas about what jobs men and women are capable of doing.

Teen 1: I don't think that is discrimination.

Teen 2: Try to be objective about this. There is plenty of evidence that women are paid less than men. Even if it's not intentional, the effects impact not only women but families too. Everyone would benefit from closing the wage gap.

Talk About It Discuss with a partner or in a group. Do you think women are treated fairly in the workplace? Why or why not? Use the sentence frame.

I think women are treated _______________________________

in the workplace because _______________________________

____.

Read the article. As you read, think about these questions:
- How has the wage gap changed over the years?
- What causes the wage gap?

Women's Wage Gap

If you were looking for a job in 1950, you would look under the heading "men's jobs" or "women's jobs" in the Help Wanted ads. The men's jobs section included management positions at higher salaries, while the "women's jobs" were all lower on the wage scale. Even if men and women held the same position, the men made more money. The difference between men and women's salaries is called a wage gap.

In the 1960s, the Equal Pay Act and Title VII were passed. The intent of these bills was to make sure men and women were treated equally in the workplace. Some say the bills helped people be more objective about gender. Others say there is evidence that discrimination still exists.

Today there is only one job section in the newspaper. Women hold management and leadership positions that were formerly reserved for men. The wage gap has gotten smaller, too. For example, in 1963 women earned 59 cents for every dollar earned by a man, but today women earn about 77–95 cents for every dollar.

Others say the gap shouldn't exist at all because by law, men and women are supposed to get equal pay for equal work. So what is the explanation for the difference? Some believe it is discrimination against women. Others point to unintentional perceptions of the jobs men and women are capable of doing. The reality is that if the wage gap closed, American families would make about $200 billion more every year.

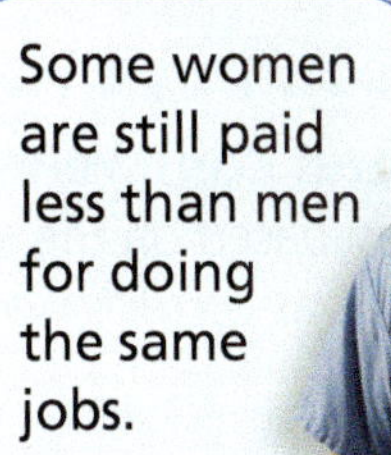

Talk About It Discuss with a partner or in a group. What do you think causes the wage gap? Try to use new vocabulary in your answer. Complete the sentence frame.

I think the wage gap is caused by ________________________

____

____.

Important Words

predict: to figure out what might happen next (*cognate: predecir*)

question: a sentence that looks for an answer

revise: to look again and correct (*cognate: revisar*)

Question Words Asking questions about details in the text can help you predict what might happen next in a particular reading. Question words consist of the following: *what, who, why, when,* and *where*. Once you have made a prediction, you can read ahead and verify or revise your prediction.

Detail:	Question:	Prediction:
Ana is happy in her new job.	Why is she happy?	She is good at her job.

Read Ahead:
Ana solved a big problem at work.

New Question:
What will her boss do?

Verify or Revise Prediction
Ana's boss will give her a raise.

Talk About It Work with a partner or in a group. Talk about what questions do. How do they help you make predictions?

- -

Extend Language and Comprehension Read the passage below. Then, make a prediction based on the information presented and verify whether the prediction was correct. Complete the chart.

Passage

Lisa was an office manager for a large company. She was one of four managers on her floor and she worked extra hours every week. Lisa worked very hard. One day, her boss mentioned that one of the managers was going to get a promotion.

Prediction: ____

Passage (continued)

Lisa was thrilled when her boss gave her the promotion after all her hard work.

Verify or Revise Prediction: _________________________________

____

Connect to Writing

Use Questions Think of all you have learned in this lesson. What new words did you use? How did you use questions to make predictions? How did you use questions to verify or revise your predictions? Talk with a partner about what you learned.

On a separate sheet of paper, write the answers to the following questions:

- How did you make predictions?
- How did you revise your predictions?

If you need help, use the sentence frames.

I made predictions by ___________________________________

____.

I revised my predictions by ________________________________

____.

Extension Activity Research

Research Report Write a research report on a career that interests you. First, decide on a career or job you would like to do to earn a living. Then, research the various types of organizations that employ people in that position. Present your results and conclusions in a coherent report.

Tips for Your Report

- Consult reliable sources for your information.
- Use facts and evidence in your report. Remember to cite both primary and secondary sources.
- Use the Writing Process Handbook at the end of this book. It will help you with prewriting, drafting, and revising.
- If you are writing on a computer, follow the directions for your word-processing program.

Vocabulary

Important Words

concrete: real or exact *(cognate: concreto)*

discern: to become aware of something that is hard to understand or see *(cognate: discernir)*

evaluate: to make a judgment about a person, place, or thing based on what you know *(cognate: evaluar)*

results: outcomes or effects *(cognate: resultados)*

uncertainty: doubt, lack of belief *(cognate: incertidumbre)*

Concept Words

happiness: to be happy

psychology: the science of how human beings feel and behave *(cognate: psicología)*

relationship: when two people feel connected to each other *(cognate: relación)*

Happiness

Dialogue

A parent and a teen are talking about relationships. Read the dialogue. Then, review the vocabulary words you read.

Teen: Dad, look at that video game. I wish I could afford to buy that system.

Parent: Why? Does playing video games by yourself make you happy?

Teen: What? Well, yeah. Besides I don't play by myself. All my friends are online playing the game with me. Why?

Parent: Well, I am just trying to discern whether or not money and things, like game systems, lead to happiness or more uncertainty in people. I just read a book that evaluates how Americans spend their time.

Teen: Oh no, not another psychology lesson.

Parent: No really, the results were very interesting! The author gives concrete proof that Americans are happier when they have good relationships with friends and family. Yet today we spend more time alone than during any other time in history.

Teen: What does this have to do with video games?

Parent: First of all, worrying about money probably makes you feel uncertain. Secondly, game systems encourage you to spend time alone. You may play the game with another person, but you are still cut off from your community. Then, when the game goes out of style, you feel anxious about getting the next popular version. Right?

Teen: Well, I hate to admit it, but you're right.

Talk About It Discuss the question with a partner or in a group. What makes you happy? Why? Use the sentence frame.

____

make(s) me happy because ___________________

____ .

Read the article. As you read, think about these questions:
• How does money impact happiness?
• How do relationships impact happiness?

Happy Together

What makes you happy? Is it money? Is it fame? Is it friends? In recent years, experts have begun to focus on the psychology of happiness. They try to discern and evaluate what makes people happy so that schools, governments, and other groups can recommend concrete ways to help people find happiness. Although the study results vary, one idea keeps showing up—people need healthy relationships to make them happy.

Some people believe money can buy them happiness, but the effect money can have on some people can be just the opposite. Studies show that money can produce happiness for people, until their basic needs are met. Then, money is no longer an important factor in their lives. In fact, money can lead to unseen consequences, like feelings of uncertainty and stress.

Studies show that close relationships with family, friends, and neighbors bring about higher rates of happiness than striving for higher incomes. Unfortunately, according to Harvard professor Robert Putnam, Americans are spending less time together and more time alone. Many adults spend long hours at work, while kids spend long hours in front of the computer or TV. To help people achieve happiness, Professor Putnam encourages people to spend more time together by joining school clubs, starting family nights, or volunteering in the community.

Studies show that close relationships are the largest cause of happiness.

Talk About It Discuss with a partner or in a group. Which relationships in your life make you the most happy? Why? Complete the sentence frame.

My relationship with _______________________________

makes me the most happy because _______________________

____.

Cause and Effect

Important Words

cause: why something happens; a reason
(*cognate: causa*)

effect: what happens next after something occurs; the result
(*cognate: efecto*)

Cause and Effect Words The article you read tells about causes and effects of happiness.

A **cause** is an event, action, or feeling that produces a result. | An **effect** is what happens as a result of a cause.

Talk About It Work with a partner. Read the chart. Circle the words that appear in the article, "Happy Together." Then, talk about how these words help you to identify cause and effect.

Cause Words	Effect Words
because	result
produce	therefore
since	consequence
cause	effect
reason	outcome

Extend Language and Comprehension To evaluate cause and effect, notice what occurs between events in the text. Did an event happen because of something else that happened before? Reflect and reread the text for details that give clues to cause and effect. Use the article, "Happy Together," to fill in the chart.

Cause: _________________________

____

____

Effect: _________________________

____

____

Cause: _________________________

____

____

Effect: _________________________

____

____

Connect to Writing

Cause and Effect Paragraph Think of all you have learned in this lesson. What new words did you use? How did you evaluate cause and effect in what you read? Talk with a partner about what you learned.

On a separate sheet of paper, write a cause and effect paragraph that answers the following questions:

- What causes did you find in the text you just read?

- What were the effects?

If you need help, use the sentence frames.

The text I read explained how ________________________________

____.

causes ____

____.

People have also discovered that ______________________________

causes ____

____.

Writing Tips

Don't forget to

1. use cause and effect words.

2. think about how details add to your information.

3. use appropriate wording for your purpose.

Extension Activity   Writing

Write a Poem On a separate sheet of paper or on a computer, write your own poem. Write about someone or something that makes you happy. What does this person or thing mean to you?

Tips for Your Poem

- Use vivid and fresh language; make elaborate comparisons.

- Be creative and artistic!

- Be careful not to lose the sense and meaning of the poem. Remember that your readers must be able to understand what you are saying.

- Read the poem aloud to yourself or to a partner. Pay attention to the rhythm and pace of your words.

- Revise your poem until you are satisfied with the way it sounds.

Lesson 4
Is there a difference between reality and truth?

Vocabulary

Important Words

approach: an organized way to do something or to get somewhere

confirm: to check to make sure something is true *(cognate: confirmar)*

objective: based on facts rather than on opinions or feelings *(cognate: objetivo)*

observe: to look at something close by or to study it *(cognate: observar)*

reality: real things, facts, or events *(cognate: realidad)*

Concept Words

endangered: in danger of becoming extinct

shudder: to shake or shiver

statistics: facts presented in number form *(cognate: estadística)*

Danger

Dialogue

Two teens are talking about sharks. Read the dialogue. Then, discuss the vocabulary words you read.

Teen 1: Do you want to go swimming at the beach later?

Teen 2: No way, not after seeing the movie, *Jaws*. I'm not swimming in the ocean anymore. Sharks are dangerous. It makes me shudder just thinking about it. Aren't you afraid of sharks?

Teen 1: No, *Jaws* isn't reality. Besides I saw a show about shark attacks. Scientists observe that sometimes sharks approach humans in the water because they mistake them for sea life.

Teen 2: Well that sounds like an objective observation, but can you confirm that I won't be attacked if I go swimming with you?

Teen 1: No, but I can tell you that statistics will show that you're more likely to die in a car accident on the way to the beach than from a shark attack. In fact, you're more of a threat to the sharks than they are to you.

Teen 2: What do you mean? I don't have big sharp teeth and I don't bite.

Teen 1: I mean you're a threat because you are human. Many sharks are becoming endangered because of human activity.

Teen 2: Well, that's good. I don't see it as any great loss.

Teen 1: I'm sure if they could, the sharks might say the same thing about you.

Talk About It Discuss the question with a partner or in a group. How would you feel if you saw a shark in the water? Why? Use the sentence frame.

I would be _______________________________________

because ____

____.

Read the article. As you read, think about these questions:
- Why are people afraid of sharks?
- What are the effects people have on sharks?

⋙ SHARK STORY ⋙

Are you afraid of sharks? Most people shudder at the mere mention of sharks, especially if they have seen the movie, *Jaws*. This 1975 film, along with its terrifying shark attacks and eerie musical score, led many people to believe shark attacks were a constant threat to humans. Some scientists believe that the film also led to the senseless killing of thousands of sharks out of fear.

Try setting your fears aside for a moment and look at the issue from an objective point of view. Reports confirm that every year only five to 10 people in the world die from shark attacks. Statistics have shown that a person is more likely to die in a car accident or from being struck by lightning. Scientists observe that most sharks only approach people because they've mistaken them for sea life, not because they want to attack humans.

Unfortunately, people are more harmful to sharks than they are to us. Humans kill millions of sharks every year for their meat and oil. Some people kill sharks for their fins. The fins are sold at a high price and are used to make shark fin soup. As a result, many varieties of sharks have become endangered. When you consider this reality, are sharks really a threat to humans, or are humans more of a threat to sharks?

Which predator is more threatening?

Talk About It Discuss the question with a partner or in a group. Do you think people cause a greater threat to sharks or do sharks cause a greater threat to people? Use examples. Complete the sentence frame.

I think ____

are more threatening because _____________________________

____.

Important Words

detail: a piece of information *(cognate: detalle)*

visualize: to create a mental picture *(cognate: visualizar)*

Visualize Details When you visualize details, you allow those details to create a picture of what you are reading. Sometimes, the mental picture you visualize can help you identify some cause and effect relationships.

Cause:	**Mental Picture:**	**Effect:**
The shark slowly approached the diver.	The shark is dangerous. The diver is scared.	The diver swims away before the shark attacks.

Talk About It Discuss the questions with a partner or in a group. Talk about the mental picture from the chart. How does it help you understand the cause? How does it help you understand the effect? Complete the sentence frame.

The mental picture helped me understand the cause and effect

because ____

____

____.

Extend Language and Comprehension Cause and effect relationships explain connections between events or details. Sometimes one cause can have several effects. Use the article, "Shark Story," to fill in the chart below. Try to create a mental picture of the cause.

Cause:
Many people saw the movie *Jaws.*

Effect: ___________________________
____
____

Effect: ___________________________
____
____

Connect to Writing

Cause and Effect Paragraph Think of all you have learned in this lesson about causes and effects. What new words did you use? How did you learn to visualize details? Talk with a partner about what you learned.

On a separate sheet of paper, write a cause and effect paragraph that answers the following questions:

- What cause had several different effects regarding how sharks are treated?

- What cause did you find that started a chain of effects? Give examples.

If you need help, use the sentence frames.

The ____

caused ____

and ____.

I also found that __________________________________

caused ____,

which then caused _________________________________.

Writing Tips

Don't forget to

1. visualize details from the article.

2. make connections between causes and effects.

3. edit for punctuation.

Connect to the Big Question

Think about all the articles you read in this unit. What article did you like best? What article did you not like? Then, think about your favorite article and say what the article was about.

Now, take some time to share your final ideas. Answer this question: How are reality and truth different?

You can complete the sentence frame below.

Reality and truth are different because _______________

____

____.

Big Question Words and Important Words

approach

comprehend

concrete

confirm

context

differentiate

discern

evaluate

evidence

improbable

intent

involve

objective

observe

perception

reality

results

subjective

uncertainty

verify

Vocabulary Review

Best Answer Read each question. Then, circle the best answer.

1. What is another word for "comprehend"?
   A. discriminate
   B. understand
   C. endanger
   D. confuse

2. You should use "subjective" to describe
   A. a position based on feelings, not facts.
   B. a feeling of being unsure of something.
   C. a fact presented in number form.
   D. a position based on facts, not opinions.

3. Which word refers to a feeling of being unsure about something?
   A. happiness
   B. objectivity
   C. reality
   D. uncertainty

4. If you "evaluate" something, you
   A. study the science of how people behave.
   B. show that something is true
   C. make judgments based on what you know.
   D. feel connected to another person.

5. What does it mean to "confirm" something?
   A. to make sure it's true
   B. to shake or shiver
   C. to become extinct
   D. to see or understand

Personal Response Complete each sentence with your response.

1. I like to observe ____

   ____.

2. The results of my last test were ______________________

   ____.

3. I like to be involved in ______________________

   ____.

4. My perception of school is different than ______________

   ____.

5. My friends can verify that I ______________________

   ____.

Comprehension Review

Make Predictions When you make a prediction, you tell what you think will happen next in a story or article based on what you already know. Read the passage below. Then, fill in the chart.

After reading about lottery winners, Roberta bought a lottery ticket at a gas station. She shoved it in her pocket, and then promptly forgot about it. Weeks later, she found the ticket before putting her clothes in the laundry. She almost threw it away, but decided to check the numbers online. As she compared the ticket to her computer screen, she began to get excited.

Story Details: ____

____

Question: ____

Background Knowledge: ____

____

Prediction: ____

Cause and Effect A cause is an event, action, or feeling that produces a result. An effect is what happens as a result of a cause. Read the passage and fill in the chart to identify cause and effect.

Alejandro loved surfing. One day, however, he a saw a shark swimming in the ocean. After that, he felt he couldn't surf or swim. He wouldn't go anywhere near the ocean. His friends and family have tried to help him overcome his fears. Now he tries to convince his friends not to surf anymore.

Cause:	Mental Picture:	Effect/Cause:	Effect:
____________ ____________ ____________	____________ ____________ ____________	____________ ____________ ____________	____________ ____________ ____________

Is there a difference between reality and truth?

In this unit, I read:

In this unit, I:

- learned new vocabulary words.
- read about different topics.
- used my background knowledge.
- used question words.
- used cause and effect words.
- visualized details.

- learned about how to make predictions.
- learned about cause and effect.
- wrote a background knowledge paragraph.
- wrote a problem and solution essay.
- wrote a research report.
- wrote a poem.

Reflection Think about what you learned in this unit. Complete each sentence frame. Share your answers with your teacher and classmates.

I wonder ____.

I learned ____.

I discovered ____.

I still want to know ____.

I still don't understand ____.

Can progress be made without conflict?

In this unit, I will read:

In this unit, I will:

- learn new vocabulary words.
- read about different topics.
- identify details.
- connect details, using my background knowledge.
- learn about questions.
- connect details to draw conclusions.
- learn how to make inferences.
- learn how to draw conclusions.
- use details.
- write a make problem and solution essay.
- write a research report.
- conduct a debate.

Can progress be made without conflict?

Connect to the Big Question

Answer these questions. Discuss your answers with your teacher and classmates.

How is progress made? What impact does conflict have on progress?

Extend the Big Question

Read each sentence frame. Write your opinions in each blank.

I think progress is made when

____
____
____
____
____
______________________________.

Conflict has impact on progress

because ______________________

____
____
____
____
______________________________.

Discuss your opinions with your teacher and classmates.

Big Question Words

Use your definitions from page 12 of the *Review and Assess* book.

adversity
(cognate: adversidad)

change

compromise
(cognate: compromise)

concession
(cognate: concesión)

confrontation
(cognate: confrontación)

debate
(cognate: debate)

motive
(cognate: motivo)

negotiate
(cognate: negociar)

oppose
(cognate: oponerse)

progress
(cognate: progreso)

radical
(cognate: radical)

reconciliation
(cognate: reconciliación)

resolve
(cognate: resolver)

struggle

unify
(cognate: unificar)

Vocabulary Workshop

Examples and Non-examples Fill in an example and a non-example for each of the Big Question Words. Follow the model.

Big Question Word	Example	Non-Example
change	the seasons	your birthday
resolve		
concession		
reconciliation		
debate		
compromise		
struggle		

The date of your birthday never changes.

Synonyms Write a word that means the same as the Big Question Word.

1. radical _______________________________________

2. unify _______________________________________

3. adversity _______________________________________

4. oppose _______________________________________

5. confrontation _______________________________________

Word Analysis

Roots A word's root can give you clues to the meaning of that word.

A root is the basic part of a word. It usually contains a word's basic meaning. Prefixes and suffixes can be added to a root to change its meaning.

The word *structure* contains the rood word *struct*. The root *struct* means "build." Using the root word, you can figure out that the word *structure* means "something that is built."

Write Words Read the roots and their meanings. Think of three words that contain each root. Use a dictionary if you need help.

Root	Meaning	Words		
magn	great			
scrib, script	to write			
ped, pod	foot			

Etymology The history of a word and its development over time is called etymology. In general, learning about the history of a word can help you remember it.

Many English words come from ancient Greek and Roman mythology. For instance, the word *muse* refers to a source of inspiration for an artist or poet. In Greek mythology, *Mousa*, or the Muses were nine sister goddesses who presided over the arts.

More Greco-Roman Words Use a dictionary to find the definitions and etymologies of the following words. Both words have their origins in Greco-Roman mythology.

Word	Definition	Etymology
narcissism		
python		

Discover Etymology Choose two Big Question Words from page 28. Write a brief summary of the word's etymology in the space below. Use a dictionary, if you need help.

Word:	Etymology:
Word:	Etymology:

Lesson 1
Can progress be made without conflict?

Vocabulary

Important Words

compromise: an agreement in which neither side gets everything it wanted

concession: something you give up, often when you don't want to *(cognate: concesión)*

confrontation: a dispute, fight, or argument *(cognate: confrontación)*

discuss: to talk about a subject

reconciliation: the act of ending a disagreement and becoming friendly again *(cognate: reconciliación)*

Concept Words

positive: describes something that is good *(cognate: positivo)*

rivalry: a strong or intense competition *(cognate: rivalidad)*

sibling: a brother or sister

Siblings

Dialogue

Two teens are talking about sibling rivalry. Read the dialogue. Then, review the vocabulary words you read.

Teen 1: Oh no, here comes my sister. We're not talking to one another today.

Teen 2: Why? What happened this time? Did you have another fight?

Teen 1: Yeah, we had another confrontation about sharing our room. I had to ask her to keep her things on her side of the room again. She ran out of the room, slammed the door, and refused to discuss it.

Teen 2: That happens with me and my brother all the time. Eventually we come to some kind of compromise. Although it involves making some concessions, it's better than staying mad at each other.

Teen 1: I don't know. My sister never has anything positive to say, and I get really tired of fighting all the time. Last month we fought almost every day over stupid things I don't even care about! It's so hard having a difficult sibling!

Teen 2: Well everyone says that some rivalry between siblings is normal, but if you're unhappy all the time, then you should talk to your parents. Maybe they can help you. Reconciliation isn't impossible.

Talk About It Discuss the questions with a partner or in a group. What do you think it means if a sibling slams the door after a confrontation? What do you think causes sibling rivalry?

Sibling rivalry is caused by ____________________________ ____ ____ .

Read the article. As you read, think about these questions:
- What positive things come from sibling rivalry?
- What can be done when rivalry becomes negative?

Siblings

Do you fight with your brother or sister? Do any of your friends fight with their **siblings**? Most brothers and sisters have **confrontations** even if they get along most of the time. Some sibling **rivalry** is unavoidable, and can even have **positive** results. There are times, however, when sibling rivalry can get out of control.

Children with siblings learn to solve problems.

What causes sibling rivalry? The reality is that all children want their parents' undivided love and attention. Having brothers and sisters requires parents and other family members to share that love and attention. When a parent appears to favor one child over the other, the situation can lead to anger and resentment. On the positive side, children with siblings learn to make **compromises** and **concessions** when a problem arises. Also, siblings may compete in ways that help them reach goals they wouldn't have acquired on their own.

In some cases, however, siblings are so angry that **reconciliation** is impossible. They are competing to hurt each other emotionally or even physically. In situations like these, parents need to **discuss** the problem with the children. When siblings learn to resolve problems together, they are building skills that will last a lifetime.

Talk About It Discuss the question with a partner or in a group. What are some positive effects of sibling rivalry? Think of at least two examples. Complete the sentence frame.

Sibling rivalry can help teens ________________________________

____

and ____.

Make Inferences

Important Words

detail: a piece
of information
(cognate: detalle)

infer: assume something
based on facts
(cognate: inferir)

Details A detail is a piece of information that acts as a clue for the reader. Details can help you infer things about what you are reading. When you make an inference, you make a logical assumption about something that you are reading.

Example: Jasmine stared angrily when she saw her sister walking towards her down the hall. Then, her sister stopped and walked away.

Details from the text:
Jasmine stared angrily.
She has a sister.
Her sister walked away to avoid Jasmine.

Talk About It Work with a partner or in a group. What can you infer from the details about how Jasmine was feeling?

Extend Language and Comprehension

Read the passage below. Look for details and use your personal experience to make inferences. Read the sentences. Then, fill in the diagram.

Brianne and her sister rode their sled together, giggling and laughing the entire way. When they reached the bottom of the hill, they both jumped up, screaming because the snow was so cold.

Story Details:		Personal Experience:		Inference:
____________	→	____________	→	____________
____________		____________		____________
____________		____________		____________
____________		____________		____________

Connect to Writing

Use Details Think of all you have learned in this lesson. What new words did you use? How did you learn to find details and use personal experience to make inferences? Talk with a partner about what you learned.

On a separate sheet of paper, write a cause and effect paragraph that answers the following questions:

- What personal experience do you have with siblings and how they get along? Give examples with details of what you have observed.

- Based on your experience, why do siblings disagree so often?

If you need help, use the sentence frames.

My personal experience is ________________________________

____ .

We / they ____ .

I think siblings fight because ______________________________

____ .

For example, ____

____ .

Extension Activity   Writing

Write a Problem and Solution Essay On a separate sheet of paper or on a computer, write a problem and solution essay about sibling rivalry. Why is it so difficult for brothers and sisters to get along? First, explain the problems that arise when brothers and sisters compete for their parents' attention. Then, think about the things that can be done to help resolve the problem, and propose your ideas as solutions.

Tips for Your Essay

- State the problem clearly.

- Propose a solution that is reasonable and practical.

- Use your own background knowledge and the details from the previous exercise to support your ideas.

- Use the Writing Process Handbook at the end of this book. This will help you with prewriting, drafting, and revising. If you are writing on a computer, follow the directions for your word-processing program.

**Lesson 2
Can progress be made without conflict?**

Vocabulary

Important Words

concession: something you give up, often when you don't want to
(cognate: concesión)

motive: a person's reason for doing something
(cognate: motivo)

produce: to make something
(cognate: producir)

progress: movement toward a goal
(cognate: progreso)

radical: extreme or very different from the usual
(cognate: radical)

Concept Words

identity: who you are
(cognate: identidad)

prevent: to keep something from happening

theft: stealing something from someone

Identity Theft

Dialogue

A teacher and a student are talking about identity theft. Read the dialogue. Then, review the vocabulary words you read.

Teacher:	What is identity theft?
Teen 1:	That's when someone steals your personal information and uses it to get things.
Teacher:	That is correct. What motive do you think identity thieves have for stealing personal information?
Teen 2:	They can steal money from your bank account or use it to get credit cards. That's what happened to my brother last year. Someone stole his identity from a website and charged over $5,000 in his name before they were caught.
Teacher:	Excellent example. There are concessions we can make to prevent this from happening. These don't have to be radical.
Teen 1:	Yes, like don't automatically trust any website or e-mail that asks you to produce personal information.
Teen 2:	My brother recommends that you make up silly user IDs on networking sites. He also says that you should never keep your social security number on your computer.
Teacher:	Great answer. We can all make progress toward preventing identify theft.

Talk About It Discuss the question with a partner or in a group. What would happen if a thief figured out your password on a website?

If an identify thief discovered my password, he or she could

____

____

_______________________________________.

Read the article. As you read, think about these questions:

- How can your identity be stolen?
- What can you do to prevent identity theft?

IDENTITY Theft

Identity theft can happen to anyone.

Imagine going to apply for a driver's license and finding out someone has already gotten a license in your name. Or imagine applying for your first credit card, only to find out you already have bad credit. These could be signs that someone has stolen your identity.

How does identity theft happen? Identity thieves use spam and "phishing" emails to steal your personal information. They can also produce email attachments containing a virus that allows them to access information on your computer. Either way, the thieves have one motive: to use your personal information to get money. They may do something as radical as steal money from your existing bank account. They may also use your information to apply for credit cards and use your name.

You can prevent this from happening by making a few basic concessions. First, never open or download anything unless it comes from a reliable source. You should only provide personal information to secure sites. Finally, when you are asked to register on personal networking sites, create a silly user ID that does not identify you. With these precautions, you can make progress toward protecting your personal information.

Talk About It Discuss the question with a partner or in a group. How does identity theft hurt the victims? Use the sentence frame.

Identity theft hurts the victims because _______________

____

_______________________________.

Important Words

infer: assume something based on facts
(cognate: inferir)

Connect Details When you infer the meaning of something you are reading, you are making a logical assumption. Making inferences helps you to understand a lot of what you are reading. When you make inferences, you will need to connect the details of what you are reading and use your background knowledge.

Example: Marcus spends all his time on the computer. He gives his personal information to any web site. His mother does not think that this is a safe idea, but Marcus does not listen to her.

Detail: Marcus gives his personal information to any web site.	**Background Knowledge:** You should give information to web sites you trust.
Detail: His mother does not think this is a safe idea.	**Background Knowledge:** Some people try to steal your information.
Detail: Marcus does not listen to her.	**Background Knowledge:** You should listen to your parents.

Inference: An identity thief might steal Marcus's information.

Talk About It Work with a partner. Discuss how you connected details and used your background knowledge to make an inference.

Extend Language and Comprehension Read the passage. Connect the details and use your background knowledge. Then, make an inference about Laura. Use the diagram to organize information.

Detail: Laura logged into her favorite networking site with the ID "LauraSmith." Her friend told her not to use her real name, so Laura changed her ID to "butterflygirl."

Background Knowledge: ____
____

Inference: ____
____

Connect to Writing

Make Inferences Paragraph Think of all you have learned in this lesson. What new words did you use? How did you learn to use details and background knowledge to make inferences? Talk with a partner about what you learned.

Now practice what you learned. On a separate sheet of paper, write a paragraph that answers the following questions:

- What background knowledge do you have about being safe on the computer? Give examples with details from your own life.

- Based on your experience and details from the article, "Identity Theft," what can you infer about identity thieves?

If you need help, use the sentence frames.

In my experience, ____

____.

For example, ____

____.

People who steal personal information probably ____________________

____.

Writing Tips

Don't forget to

1. use background knowledge.

2. make inferences about information in the article.

3. revise your writing for sentence structure.

Extension Activity   Research

Research Report Write a research report on identity theft. Investigate the possible ways that thieves can gain access to your personal and financial information. Analyze your findings, come to a conclusion, and offer some advice on how we can protect ourselves.

Tips for Your Report

- Consult reliable sources for your information.

- Use the inferences you made in the previous exercise to help you think about this essay.

- Support your opinion with facts and evidence. Remember to cite both primary and secondary sources.

- Use the Writing Process Handbook at the end of this book. This will help you with prewriting, drafting, and revising. If you are writing on a computer, follow the directions for your word-processing program.

**Lesson 3
Can progress be made without conflict?**

Vocabulary

Important Words

conclude: to use clues to figure out something not stated; to form an opinion based on evidence *(cognate: concluir)*

debate: a discussion of arguments in favor of and against a certain action *(cognate: debate)*

former: when something already happened or existed in the past

negotiate: to agree through discussion and compromise *(cognate: negociar)*

resolve: to deal with a problem successfully by fixing it *(cognate: resolver)*

Concept Words

advertising: the display of products on the radio, or television, or in stores which makes people want to buy them

greed: an intense desire to have a lot of money or own a lot of things

materialistic: when you want to buy and own things *(cognate: materialista)*

Greed

Dialogue

Two teens are talking about advertising and shopping. Read the dialogue. Then, review the vocabulary words you read.

Teen 1: Let's go shopping! Last night I saw a commercial for a pair of jeans that I have to buy. I also need a new pair of shoes. This pair is so out of style.

Teen 2: Listen to yourself! When did you become so materialistic? You have been completely fooled by advertising.

Teen 1: What do you mean? There is really no debate here. I don't have a lot of greed. I just know what I like and what I want.

Teen 2: Yes, but you don't need any of it. Take your shoes for example. They look fine to me. What made you conclude that you needed new ones?

Teen 1: Well, I saw the newest style on TV which made me realize mine were old. I can't really afford them, but I've resolved the problem by negotiating with my mom to do extra chores for the money.

Teen 2: Do you remember your former self? When we were kids you didn't care about popular jeans and shoes, and you were happier.

Teen 1: Yes, but I was not the most popular girl then!

Talk About It Discuss the questions with a partner or in a group. Do your clothes make you who you are? Why? Use the sentence frame.

I think clothes ___________________________________

____

because ____

____.

Read the article. As you read, think about these questions:
- How do advertisements impact your decisions?
- How does the topic of the article relate to the topic of the dialogue?

THE GREED GAME

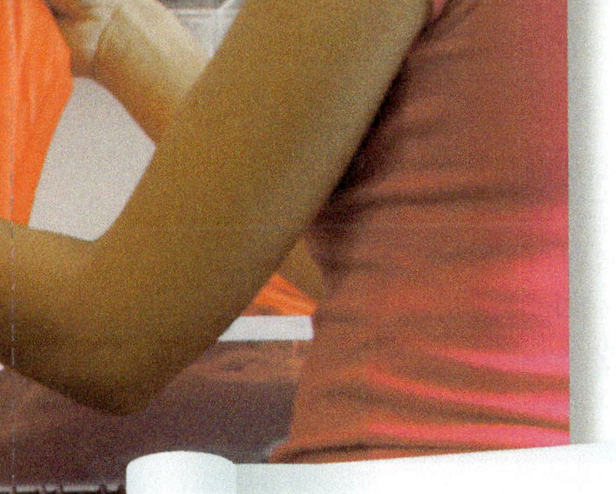

Does **advertising** affect your life? Think about the clothes and products you want. Do you look for brand names that are popular? Do you think you need things to be considered popular or in style? These questions are at the center of a **debate** over teen buying habits. Some people believe teens have become overly **materialistic** and are always wanting and spending more than they can afford. Others **conclude** that teens are victims of advertisers who are focused on **greed**. These advertisers look to make a profit off teens because today they are the hottest consumer buying group in the nation.

In **former** years, advertisers ignored this age group, but today teens spend about $100 billion a year. Today advertisers study ways to appeal to teens. They often prey on insecurities about appearance, being popular, and finding happiness. Instead of informing people about a product, most ads give false promises, such as, "If you wear these jeans, you'll be popular." Unfortunately, these ads do not help teens **resolve** any of their problems. They only make teens frustrated, anxious, and lonely because the underlying message is you need to keep buying things or you're not good enough. Consequently, teens have a reputation for always wanting more.

How do you **negotiate** between what you want and what you need? One teen knew he had to change his spending habits after he got a job and realized the value of money.

What underlying messages does advertising send?

Talk About It Discuss with a partner or in a group. Do you think teens are overly materialistic or are they the victims of advertising? Complete the sentence frame.

I think ____

____

because ____

____.

Important Words

conclude to form an opinion based on evidence (*cognate: concluir*)

question: a sentence that looks for an answer

support: to provide evidence for something

Question Words Asking questions about details in the text can help you to conclude the point of a particular reading. Question words consist of the following: *what, who, why, when, where,* and *how*. The answers to your questions support your conclusions.

Detail: One teen resolved to change his spending habits.

Detail: He got a job to earn money.

Question: How did the job help the teen change his spending habits?

Conclusion: The teen learned to be responsible about money.

Talk About It Work with a partner or in a small group. Talk about what questions do. How do they help you draw conclusions about what you are reading?

Extend Language and Comprehension When you **draw conclusions**, you connect details to create an overall idea of what you read. Asking questions and organizing the information can help to clarify your thinking. Reread the article, "The Greed Game." Then, use the diagram to connect details and draw a conclusion.

Detail	
Detail	
Detail	
Conclusion	

Connect to Writing

Use Questions Think of all you have learned in this lesson. What new words did you use? How did you use questions to find details? How did you draw conclusions? Talk with a partner about what you learned.

On a separate sheet of paper, write the answers to the following questions:

- What questions did you use as you read "The Greed Game"?
- How did the questions help you find details?
- What conclusions did you draw from "The Greed Game"?

If you need help, use the sentence frames.

One question I used as I read "The Greed Game" was ______________

____.

This question helped me because ______________________________

____.

The conclusion I drew was ____________________________________

____.

Extension Activity   Listening and Speaking

Conduct a Debate Discuss with some of your classmates the issue of teens and advertising. Do you think teens are overly materialistic? Or do you think advertisers take advantage of them? Consider the evidence and decide what you think. Then, divide into teams and debate your opinions with your classmates.

Tips for Your Debate

- State your opinions in a clear way; try to choose the right word.
- Use facts and examples to support your opinions.
- Consider the best way to convince your opponents. How would you win them over to your side? With logic? With emotion?
- Think about the questions you raised and the conclusions you drew in the previous exercise.
- Be prepared for your opponent's arguments and have counter-arguments ready.
- Remember to keep a cool head in your heated debate!

**Lesson 4
Can progress be made without conflict?**

Vocabulary

Important Words

motive: a person's reason for doing something
(*cognate: motivo*)

negotiate: to agree through discussion and compromise
(*cognate: negociar*)

resolve: to deal with a problem successfully by fixing it
(*cognate: resolver*)

unify: to bring people or things together
(*cognate: unificar*)

Concept Words

development: when something gets bigger, fuller, or better

protect: to shield someone or something from danger or injury
(*cognate: proteger*)

sprawl: to spread out without any control

Land Development

Dialogue

A teacher and two students are talking about land development. Read the dialogue. Then, review the vocabulary words you read.

Teacher:	Today we're talking about land **development**. Who can give me an example of what that is?
Teen 1:	My dad complains a lot about suburban **sprawl**. Is that land development?
Teacher:	That is an excellent example. Suburban sprawl is a type of development that uses up open spaces. What **motive** might people have to protest against this type of development?
Teen 2:	They probably want to **protect** the open spaces.
Teacher:	Yes, that is one reason. Another reason is that living in the suburbs can cost taxpayers more money in property taxes. Do you know why?
Teen 1:	My dad says that some developers never **resolve** the problem of transportation, and that suburbs require new roads, water, and sewage systems to be built. All of that costs taxpayers money.
Teacher:	Exactly. What rights do you think residents should have when developers decide to change their communities?
Teen 2:	I think they should be able to **unify** themselves and **negotiate** with developers about changes that will affect their community.

Talk About It Discuss the questions with a partner or in a group. Do you think there should be rules regarding land development? Circle your opinion. Then, fill in the sentence frame.

I think there should/should not be rules regarding

development because ___________________________________

____

____.

Read the article. As you read, think about these questions:
- Why is land development a cause of debate?
- How is the topic of the article related to the topic of the dialogue?

THE DEVELOPMENT DEBATE

Have you ever thought about the way land **development** changes the character of a community? When a vacant lot is turned into an office building or new apartments, the community benefits from new jobs or housing. On the other hand, when a developer destroys a park to build new homes, a community suffers from a lack of open space.

The **motive** behind developers' preference to build on open spaces is to save money and trouble. It's easier to develop on open land than in cities.

According to the American Farmland Trust, more than six million acres of farmland in the U.S. were turned into suburban developments in just five years. Suburban **sprawl** takes people farther outside the city. This causes people to drive long distances for work and leisure. Taxpayers must also pay more, because basic services like water and sewage have to be built from scratch.

Developers say these sacrifices are necessary in order to accommodate

Most suburbs are built on farmland and other open spaces.

the growing U.S. population. However, others argue that developing high density housing in the cities would **protect** open spaces and utilize services that already exist.

When developers begin planning, many residents feel they should have the right to **negotiate** with them. Residents often **resolve** to control land development by **unifying** to protect their community.

Talk About It Discuss with a partner or in a group. Do you think developers should build more in the suburbs or the cities? Why? Complete the sentence frame.

I think developers should build more in _______________________

because ____

____.

Important Words

conclude to form an opinion based on evidence
(cognate: concluir)

connect: to show how things are related
(cognate: conectar)

detail: a piece of information
(cognate: detalle)

infer: assume something based on facts
(cognate: inferir)

Connect Details A detail is a piece of information in the form of a word or sentence that acts as a clue. You can infer the meaning of something when you analyze and connect details. This will help you to conclude whether or not something is important.

Example:
Margie stomped into the suburban land development meeting and demanded to speak with the person in charge.

Details from the text:
Margie stomped into the meeting.
She demanded to speak to the person in charge.
The meeting is about suburban land development.

Talk About It Discuss the question with a partner or in a group. Analyze the details. What do these details tell you about Margie? Analyze and connect the details to draw a conclusion.

Extend Language and Comprehension Connect details from the article "The Development Debate" to draw a conclusion. Fill in the chart below.

Detail: _______________________

____

____

Detail: _______________________

____

____

Detail: _______________________

____

____

Conclusion: _______________________

____

____

____

____

____

Connect to Writing

Draw Conclusions Paragraph Think of all you have learned in this lesson. What new words did you use? How did you learn to analyze details and draw conclusions? Talk with a partner about what you learned.

On a separate sheet of paper, write a paragraph that answers the following questions:

- How did you find details?
- How did you analyze the details?
- How did you draw conclusions?

If you need help, use the sentence frames.

> To find the details ____
>
> ____ .
>
> Then, I analyzed them by _______________________________
>
> ____ .
>
> I drew conclusions by __________________________________
>
> ____ .

Connect to the Big Question 

Think about all the articles you read in this unit. What article did you like best? What article did you not like? Then, think about your favorite article and say what the article was about.

Now, take some time to share your final ideas. Answer this question: What type of progress can conflict bring?

You can complete the sentence frame below.

> Conflict can bring progress when ___________________________
>
> ____
>
> ____ .

Big Question Words and Important Words

adversity

change

compromise

concession

conclude

confrontation

debate

discuss

former

motive

negotiate

oppose

produce

progress

radical

reconciliation

resolve

struggle

unify

Vocabulary Review

Best Definition Read the sentence. Circle the best definition for each underlined word.

1. To get along, my sister and I learned to make <u>concessions</u>.
   A. confrontations
   B. snacks
   C. arguments
   D. compromises

2. She tried to <u>unify</u> her siblings.
   A. create a dispute
   B. form an opinion
   C. bring together
   D. talk about something

3. I had a good <u>motive</u> for wanting the clothes.
   A. reason
   B. discussion
   C. compromise
   D. struggle

4. I ran into my <u>former</u> teacher in the grocery store.
   A. current
   B. past
   C. future
   D. foreign

5. It took a long time to <u>resolve</u> the argument.
   A. unify
   B. settle
   C. produce
   D. confront

Write Sentences Write a sentence for each word.

1. compromise ___________________________________

   ____.

2. debate ______________________________________

   ____.

3. oppose ______________________________________

   ____.

4. reconciliation ________________________________

   ____.

5. struggle _____________________________________

   ____.

Make Inferences An inference is an assumption you make about a detail you read. You make inferences by connecting details in what you are reading with your background knowledge. Read the passage below. Then, complete the chart.

> Martin was unfamiliar with computers. He didn't know how to update the antivirus software. He spent a few hours one evening surfing the Internet. Some of the sites he visited were safe. He found other sites by accident. The next day, Martin was shocked to find his computer had a virus. He was worried.

Story Details:

____

____

____

____

____

Personal Experience:

____

____

____

____

____

Inference:

____

____

____

____

____

Draw Conclusions When you draw a conclusion, you reach a decision or opinion about what you have read. Use the diagram to connect details and to draw conclusions about the topic.

> Alicia usually watched TV after school. Then, she would play basketball with her friends. Today, she jumped up after watching TV and begged her mom for some money to buy new basketball shoes. "What for?" her mom replied, "I bought you new shoes a few months ago." Alicia explained that she just saw a commercial for the latest basketball shoes. The commercial said that the shoes could make a basketball player fly.

Detail: ______________________

____

____

Detail: ______________________

____

____

Question:
Will Alicia's mom buy her new basketball shoes? Why?

Conclusion: ______________________

____

____

____

Can progress be made without conflict?

In this unit, I read:

In this unit, I:

- learned new vocabulary words.
- read about different topics
- identified details.
- connected details, using my background knowledge.
- learned about questions.
- connected details to draw conclusions.

- learned how to make inferences.
- learned how to draw conclusions.
- used details.
- wrote a problem and solution essay.
- wrote a research report.
- conducted a debate.

Reflection Think about what you learned in this unit. Complete each sentence frame. Share your answers with your teacher and classmates.

I wonder ____.

I learned ____.

I discovered ____.

I still want to know ____.

I still don't understand ____.

What kind of knowledge changes our lives?

In this unit, I will read:

In this unit, I will:

- learn new vocabulary words.
- read about different topics.
- use supporting details.
- learn about implied details and stated details.
- use persuasive words.
- use persuasive techniques.
- learn about the main idea.
- learn about persuasive appeals.
- write a main idea outline.
- write a persuasive essay.
- write a main idea paragraph.
- write a descriptive essay.
- write persuasive paragraphs.

What kind of knowledge changes our lives?

Connect to the Big Question
Answer these questions. Discuss your answers with your teacher and classmates.

What types of knowledge are there? Which types of knowledge affect you most?

Extend the Big Question
Read each sentence frame. Write your opinions in each blank.

One type of knowledge is

____
____
____
_______________________.

Another type of knowledge is

____
____
____
_______________________.

I am most affected by _________
____
____
_______________________.

Discuss your opinions with your teacher and classmates.

Big Question Words

Use your definitions from page 23 of the *Review and Assess* book.

adapt
(cognate: adaptar)

awareness

empathy
(cognate: empatía)

enlighten

evolve
(cognate: evolucionar)

growth

history
(cognate: historia)

ignorance
(cognate: ignorancia)

influence
(cognate: influencia)

insight

modified
(cognate: modificado)

question
(cognate: questionar)

reflect
(cognate: reflexionar)

revise
(cognate: revisar)

understanding

Vocabulary Workshop

Answer the Questions Read each question. Then, write the Big Question Word that best answers each question.

1. What word describes what happened in the past?
   ____

2. What word means almost the same as "to challenge"?
   ____

3. What word describes something slightly changed?
   ____

4. What word means nearly the opposite of "knowledgeable"?
   ____

5. What word means almost the same as "development"?
   ____

Use Context Fill in the lines with Big Question Words.

Our project is due tomorrow, and we have to

_______________________ it quite a bit if we want a good

grade. I was convinced that we needed a poster, but Ally

began to _______________________ that suggestion when

she reread the assignment. I reread it, too. After I took some

time to _______________________ on what Professor Schmidt

wanted, my knowledge, or _______________________, of

the project changed. Ally and I stayed up all night working

on the project. We're hoping it is better, and it will

_______________________ our

We both want to get that A!

Prefixes Prefixes can give you clues about the meaning of words. A prefix is a group of letters that appear at the beginning of a word. A prefix can help form a new word.

For example, the prefix *mis-* means "wrongly" or "opposite of". You can add the prefix *mis-* to the word interpret to form the word "misinterpret".

mis- + interpret = misinterpret

wrongly + interpret = to interpret wrongly

Make New Words Use the prefixes listed below to make new words. Use a dictionary to check your spelling.

Prefix	New Word
mis-	
un-	

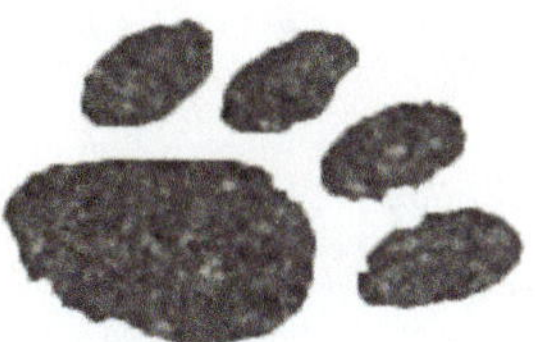

We misinterpreted these animal prints.

Choose one of the new words. Then, write the word and its definition. Use a dictionary if you need help.

My Word: ____

Definition: ____

Many English (and Spanish) words contain prefixes with Greek and Latin origins. Knowing the meaning of these prefixes can help you remember the meanings of words.

For example, the prefix *pre-* is from *præ* in Latin which means "before". So, the word *preview* means "view before". When you *preview* a book, you are looking at it before you read it.

Write Words Look at the prefixes in the chart below. Write two words that contain the prefix. You can use a dictionary to help you.

Prefix	Meaning	New Words	
post	after		
trans	across		
re	again		
tri	three		

Lesson 1
What kind of knowledge changes our lives?

Vocabulary

Important Words

awareness: knowledge that something exists

distinguish: to tell the difference between similar things (*cognate: distinguir*)

evolve: to slowly improve over time (*cognate: evolucionar*)

insight: a clear understanding

reaction: a particular behavior in response to something (*cognate: reacción*)

Concept Words

instinct: a natural reaction to something (*congate: instinto*)

intuition: a very quick and strong insight (*cognate: intuición*)

mechanism: a process, technique or system that helps you achieve something (*cognate: mecanismo*)

Intuition

Dialogue

Two teens are discussing the "sixth sense." Read the dialogue. Then, review the vocabulary words you read.

Teen 1: I heard you were in a car accident yesterday. Are you okay?

Teen 2: Yeah, I'm fine.

Teen 1: What happened?

Teen 2: Well, I had an instinct or funny feeling when I jumped into my sister's car. I forgot to buckle my seat belt. Then I got this weird feeling, so I put it on. It was my intuition talking. One minute later, a driver, coming in the opposite direction, skidded out of control and crashed into us!

Teen 1: Wow, it's lucky you listened to your intuition. Your reaction saved your life. I hope I have that kind of insight or awareness if I'm in a situation like that.

Teen 2: Well, we've all evolved to have the same "sixth sense" mechanism. Some people just pay more attention to it than others.

Teen 1: I guess I'm not sure if I can distinguish between feelings that are just silly fears and feelings of real danger.

Teen 2: I think it's better to be safe than sorry. If you have a strange feeling, you should pay attention to it. I'm proof that the "sixth sense" can save your life.

Talk About It Discuss the questions with a partner or in a small group. Do you sometimes get a feeling that something is going to happen? How do you respond to it? Complete the sentence frame.

When I get a feeling that something is going to happen, I

____

because _______________________________________.

Read the article. As you read, think about these questions:
- What is the "sixth sense"?
- How does the topic of the article relate to the topic of the dialogue?

Sixth Sense Survival

Have you ever had a funny or uneasy feeling you just couldn't explain? Was the feeling telling you something bad was going to happen? A young teenager in Mississippi got this feeling while riding with her friends in a car. She realized that she had forgotten to fasten her seat belt and put it on. Minutes later, the driver lost control of the car and crashed. The emergency workers said the seat belt saved the girl's life.

Some people call this feeling intuition. Others call it a survival instinct or a "sixth sense." Researchers say it is a mechanism in the brain that triggers a reaction to small clues in the environment. According to the researchers, this mechanism may have evolved from a type of awareness humans used thousands of years ago to help them survive. They used this awareness to help them distinguish between dangerous and safe surroundings. In today's world, we may be out of practice, but the instinct remains.

So how does it work? One professor's research has given him many insights on the sixth sense. He believes the sixth sense is related to two types of vision — conscious and unconscious. Those people who develop a "sixth sense" may not be aware that they are picking up changes in the environment, although this is why they are able to predict danger before it happens. The trick is to pay attention to your feelings and believe in them.

Talk About It Discuss the questions with a partner or in a small group. Do you think the "sixth sense" is something real or imaginary? Why? Circle your opinion. Then, complete the sentence frame.

I think the "sixth sense" is/is not real because ________________

____

____.

Important Words

main idea: the topic

supporting detail: information that helps you understand the main idea or topic

Supporting Details The main idea of an article or passage is its topic, or the most important thing an author wants to say. Supporting details are the words and sentences an author uses to explain his or her main idea. Without supporting details, the reader would have a hard time understanding the author's thoughts.

In the paragraph below, the main idea is in **bold**. A supporting detail is <u>underlined</u>.

What is the "sixth sense?" **It is an important mechanism humans use to detect danger.** Historically, humans used this instinct to survive in the wild. Today we often ignore it by saying, "Oh, I just have an overactive imagination." However, researchers have gained new insights into how it works. <u>They think the "sixth sense" can actually save lives.</u>

Talk About It Discuss the paragraph above with a partner or in a small group. Look at all the sentences. Underline sentences that most directly support the main idea. Circle sentences that do not directly support the main idea.

Extend Language and Comprehension Read the passage below. What is the main idea? What supporting details can you find? Complete the chart.

It's a common experience. You get the feeling that someone is watching you. Then, you look around and discover that there is someone watching you. Some people would say that this is only one example of your sixth sense at work. They think that all of us have a sixth sense, but that we have gotten out of practice using it. Do you use your sixth sense?

Main Idea: ____

____

Supporting Detail: _______________________________________

____

____

Connect to Writing

Main Idea Outline Think of all you have learned in this lesson. What new words did you use? How did you learn to find supporting details and the main idea? Talk with a partner about what you learned.

Write a paragraph that explains your own thoughts about people having a "sixth sense." Make sure to answer the following questions:

- What is your main idea?

- What are four key details that support your main idea?

If you need help organizing your thoughts, use the outline below.

Outline

Main Idea: ____

Supporting details:

1.____

2.____

3.____

4.____

Writing Tips

Don't forget to

1. create a clear main idea for your paragraph.

2. think of examples, explanations, or reasons that support your main idea.

3. use effective transitions.

Extension Activity   Writing

Write an Essay Write an essay about the "sixth sense." Do you believe some (or all) people have it? Why or why not? Think of examples and details, and try to convince your readers.

Tips for Your Essay

- Develop your essay from the main idea outline you wrote in the previous exercise.

- State your descriptions and opinions clearly.

- Support your opinions with details.

- Try to include other opinions that do not support yours. Then, show why you disagree with these opinions. This will help you present a full picture of the issues.

- Use the Writing Process Handbook at the end of this book. This will help you with prewriting, drafting, and revising. If you are writing on a computer, follow the directions for your word-processing program.

Lesson 2
What kind of knowledge changes our lives?

Vocabulary

Important Words

influence: the effect of something on a person, a thing, or an event (*cognate: influencia*)

process: a series of steps taken to do a task or meet a goal (*cognate: proceso*)

question: a sentence that looks for an answer

reflect: to think calmly and carefully (*cognate: reflexionar*)

statement: an expression of an idea or opinion

Concept Words

dress code: a set of rules that say what people can wear in a specific place, like a school

extreme: much more than ordinary, usual or expected (*cognate: extremo*)

squelch: to not allow something to happen

Dress Codes

Dialogue

A teacher is discussing a new dress code with the class. Read the dialogue. Then, review the vocabulary words you read.

Teacher: By now you've all heard about the new dress code. Are there any questions?

Student 1: I have reflected on the issue. I'm really angry about it. I have a right to wear what I want.

Student 2: Yeah, but some of your fashion statements can be pretty extreme. That day you wore safety pins in your ears I couldn't concentrate.

Student 1: I'm not forcing you to look at me. So why are you trying to squelch my right to express myself? It's a matter of free speech.

Teacher: The school decided to take action only if one student's clothing distracts another student's learning process.

Student 1: I bet they didn't involve any students in making that decision.

Student 2: Actually, there were several students who supported dress codes.

Teacher: There is a national trend toward dress codes today. Schools have found that clothing has an influence on student behavior. In schools with dress codes there are fewer fights.

Talk About It Discuss the question with a partner or in a small group. What do you think about dress codes? Why? Complete the sentence frame.

I think dress codes are _______________________

because _______________________

____

Read the article. As you read, think about these questions:
- What are the arguments for and against dress codes?
- How does the topic of the article relate to the topic of the dialogue?

Dressing by the Book

Do you think students have a right to dress however they want? What if a student's fashion ==statement== creates a negative learning environment for other students? These questions are at the heart of the ==dress code== debate in schools around the country.

People support dress codes for a number of reasons. Many parents and students want rules that restrict gang colors or symbols in school. To them, clothing has become a safety issue. Others support rules that restrict ==extreme== fashion statements such as body piercing, tattoos, and clothes that distract other students from the ==process== of learning. To these people, school is like the workplace, and dress codes are a fact of life. Schools that have adopted dress codes report lower levels of conflict among students and improved learning conditions. These things indicate that dress codes have an ==influence== on behavior.

Some schools require all students wear uniforms.

People also oppose dress codes for a number of reasons. Some believe students have a right to wear clothes that show their personal style, and that dress codes ==squelch== individuality. Others, including the American Civil Liberties Union, believe it is an issue of free speech. They have raised ==questions== regarding the rights of schools to limit personal expression.

While people ==reflect== on the issue and the debate rages on, about half of the U.S. schools have decided to enforce strict dress codes.

Talk About It Discuss the question with a partner or a small group. Do you think dress codes limit a student's right to free speech? Circle your opinion. Then, complete the sentence frame.

I do/do not believe that school dress codes limit a student's

right to free speech because ___________________________________

____.

Important Words

implied: not expressed directly

main idea: the topic

stated: expressed directly

Implied vs. Stated Main Idea The main idea is the most important thing an author wants to say. It is the central message of the text.

Sometimes, a piece of writing will include a main idea that is stated. When a main idea is stated, you can easily identify it in the text. In other instances, the main idea is not stated. When a main idea is not stated, it means you have to use supporting details to identify it. A main idea that is not stated is called an implied main idea.

This chart contains examples of each kind of main idea.

Stated Main Idea	Implied Main Idea
This article is about the debate about dress codes. Some schools have dress codes. Other schools do not.	Some people believe dress codes are good for school safety. Other people believe dress codes hurt student expression.

Talk About It Discuss the chart with a partner or in a small group. Then, explain the difference between stated and implied main ideas in your own words.

Extend Language and Comprehension Reread "Dressing By the Book" on page 59. Think of the article's main idea. Then, complete the chart. Add details to support the main idea. Then, decide if the main idea is stated or implied.

Some people think dress codes help make schools safer.

Main Idea

Some people think dress codes deny students the right to free speech.

Connect to Writing

Main Idea Paragraph Think of all you have learned in this lesson. What new words did you use? How did you learn to distinguish between implied and stated main ideas? How did you find the main idea? Talk with a partner about what you learned.

Now, write your own paragraph. Use the topic of school dress codes. Think of your main idea and supporting details. On a separate sheet of paper, make sure to include

- a clear main idea.

- at least three supporting details.

If you need help, use the sentence frames.

Dress codes are ____

____.

For example, ____

____.

This has reduced ____

____.

As a result, ____

____.

Writing Tips
Don't forget to

1. think of why you are including details.

2. make sure the details support the main idea.

3. use effective transitions.

Extension Activity   Writing

Write a Descriptive Essay On a separate sheet of paper or on a computer, describe your ideal school uniform. Describe what it would look like and how it would appeal to everyone in the school. Explain why you made the choices you did.

Tips for Your Essay

- Remember that this is not just *your* uniform, and that everyone in the school will be wearing something similar.

- Use vivid and expressive language.

- Be reasonable. Be aware of your school's current dress guidelines.

- Use the Writing Process Handbook at the end of this book. This will help you with prewriting, drafting, and revising. If you are writing on a computer, follow the directions for your word-processing program.

Vocabulary

Important Words

empathy: understanding and sharing another person's feelings
(cognate: empatía)

evolve: to slowly improve over time
(cognate: evolucionar)

question: to challenge the truth of something
(cognate: cuestionar)

represent: to act out the example of something
(cognate: representar)

revise: to make corrections to something in order to improve it
(cognate: revisar)

Concept Words

dilemma: a very difficult and unpleasant choice
(cognate: dilema)

obligation: a duty; something you need to do
(cognate: obligación)

witness: someone who sees something and reports it

Witnesses and Responsibility

Dialogue

Two lawyers are discussing a witness in a court case. Read the dialogue. Then, review the vocabulary words you read.

Lawyer 1: How is your case proceeding?

Lawyer 2: Slowly, I'm still trying to get my witness to testify.

Lawyer 1: What's preventing her from testifying? She has a moral obligation to help solve the crime.

Lawyer 2: Well, I have empathy for her. The case represents a major dilemma for her. She questions our ability to keep her safe.

Lawyer 1: Why? Doesn't she know the law protects witnesses?

Lawyer 2: Yes, but she is afraid the criminal will seek revenge in the future. Because she is afraid, she revised her testimony the last time we talked.

Lawyer 1: That's difficult. Do you have any other witnesses?

Lawyer 2: No. Someone called a tip into the state crime hotline. This helped detectives solve the case, but it doesn't help me in court. I can't use information that is provided anonymously.

Lawyer 1: How can the justice system evolve, or survive, for that matter, if no one is willing to testify?

Lawyer 2: That's a good question.

Talk About It Discuss the questions with a partner or in a small group. Imagine you witnessed a crime. Would you feel obligated to testify? Why or why not? Circle your opinion. Then, complete the sentence frame.

I would/would not feel obligated to testify because __________

____

____.

Read the article. As you read, think about these questions:
- What dilemmas do witnesses face?
- How can the justice system better protect witnesses?

The Witness Dilemma

Imagine you have just witnessed a violent crime. Now you face a **dilemma**. You have **empathy** for the victim. You also feel the moral **obligation** to help law enforcement catch the criminal. On the other hand, you **question** the wisdom of getting involved. What if the criminal wants revenge? What if the trial turns into a long, drawn-out legal process?

Witnesses **represent** an important part of the legal system and they need to do their part. A **witness** can make the difference between justice for the victim and a criminal going free. However, the choice to get involved is not always easy. Many witnesses are frightened to speak up. Some **revise** their testimony to avoid facing revenge from angry criminals. Others worry about losing their jobs if they take the time to go through a trial.

The witness dilemma is a serious one and a partial solution has begun to **evolve** in some states. Law enforcement agencies in these states have set up hot lines where a witness can remain anonymous while calling in to report a crime. However, witnesses must be willing to speak up, and sometimes go to court, if our system of justice is to survive and justice is to be done.

Talk About It How can the justice system better protect witnesses of serious crime? Use the sentence frame.

To protect witnesses, I think the justice system should ___________

____

____

____.

Important Words

logical: makes sense
(cognate: lógico)

persuasive appeals: the arguments an author makes

Persuasive Words Some authors use persuasive words to convince the reader of their beliefs or opinions. To evaluate an author's claims, check to see if the author's persuasive appeals, or arguments, are supported by facts. If they are not supported by facts, then the claims are not logical.

This chart contains examples of some persuasive sentences and persuasive words.

Author's Position	Persuasive Words
I feel that the justice system must find better ways to protect witnesses.	feel, must
It is clear that there is only one solution to the problem: witnesses should no longer testify in court.	clear, only, should

Talk About It Work with a partner or in a group. Discuss the two sentences in the chart. Why are the sentences persuasive? Can you support the claims with facts?

• •

Extend Language and Comprehension Read the following passage. Then, fill in the chart. Write the author's claim. Then, list two examples that support the claim.

I strongly believe that witnesses should not always have to testify in court. Some people say that witnesses are the only thing standing between justice and a criminal walking free, but this just isn't true. For example, physical evidence like DNA testing can be even more reliable than a witness. Also, witnesses must think about their own safety. If they have to testify in front of a dangerous criminal, they may be threatened later. Finally, witnesses are not treated well by the justice system. Can you believe that, in some states, witnesses are even held in jail until the trial is over!

Claim: ____

____

Support: ____

____

Support: ____

____

Persuasive Paragraph Think of all you have learned in this lesson. What new words did you use? How did you learn to identify and analyze persuasive appeals? Talk with a partner about what you learned.

On a separate sheet of paper, use the topic of "The Witness Dilemma" to write a persuasive paragraph. Make sure to answer the following questions:

- What is your position?
- What claims support your position?
- What facts or evidence support your claims?

If you need help, use the sentence frames.

Witnesses should/should not testify in court because ______________

____

____.

The facts show ____.

Therefore ____.

Extension Activity   Writing

Write an Essay Write an essay about witness responsibility. Should people that have witnessed a crime be forced to testify? Do they have a moral responsibility? Or, might there be good reasons for them to refuse? Come to a conclusion and try to persuade your readers.

Tips for Your Essay

- Develop your essay from the persuasive paragraph you wrote in the exercise above.
- State your descriptions and opinions clearly.
- Support your opinions with facts and other evidence.
- Try to include other opinions that do not support yours. Then, show why you disagree with these opinions. This will help you present a full picture of the issues.
- Use the Writing Process Handbook at the end of this book. This will help you with prewriting, drafting, and revising. If you are writing on a computer, follow the directions for your word-processing program.

Lesson 4
What kind of knowledge changes our lives?

Vocabulary

Important Words

adapt: to change in order to fit a new situation (cognate: adaptar)

argument: a reason that is given to support or oppose a point of view (cognate: argumento)

empathy: understanding and sharing another person's feelings (cognate: empatía)

ignorance: lack of knowledge about something (cognate: ignorancia)

understanding: a knowledge of what something means

Concept Words

freedom: the power to act, speak, or think as one chooses

immigrant a person who comes to a new country in order to live there (cognate: inmigrante)

opportunity: a good chance to advance or progress (cognate: oportunidad)

Freedoms

Dialogue

A teacher is discussing immigration with some students. Read the dialogue. Then, review the vocabulary words you read.

Teacher: Today, we're talking about why people immigrate to the United States. Who can give me some reasons?

Student 1: I think some people come for the opportunity to have a different kind of life. Others are looking for freedom.

Teacher: Immigrants have many different reasons for coming to the United States. Can anyone think of another reason why someone might immigrate?

Student 2: My father is from Vietnam. He came here to escape religious persecution but found it difficult to adapt. He said few people showed any understanding or empathy for his experience.

Teacher: Yes, relating to strangers can be a struggle for many immigrants. One argument is that people who are raised in the United States don't understand the cultures of immigrants. There is some ignorance about culture.

Student 1: One positive thing, though, is freedom. We have different kinds of freedom in the United States such as freedom of speech or freedom from want. I think many immigrants come seeking many different kinds of freedom.

Teacher: I think we can all agree that immigrants may face challenges, but freedoms can make it worthwhile.

Talk About It Discuss the question with a partner or in a small group. Is everyone in the United States afforded the same freedoms? Circle your opinion. Then, complete the sentence frame.

I think everyone (is/is not) afforded the same freedoms

because ____

____.

Read the article. As you read, think about these questions:
- Why do immigrants come to the United States?
- What freedoms exist in the United States?

The Newest Newcomers

The United States is still a nation of immigrants.

The United States began as a nation of ==immigrants==. Early colonists came to America for the ==opportunity== to start anew in a land that promised religious ==freedom==. The challenges they faced trying to ==adapt== to a new land were tremendous.

Today, we are still a nation of immigrants. Millions of immigrants come to the United States every year. Like the earliest immigrants, some still come seeking religious freedom. In the United States they are free to worship without fear. However, most immigrants today come to America for a variety of other reasons. But like the first immigrants, they face many of the same heartbreaking challenges.

Modern immigrants put themselves through the struggle of dealing with the cultural ==ignorance== some strangers have. Some people have little ==understanding== or ==empathy== for the hardships immigrants face. So why do modern immigrants come to America?

A recent television program presented the ==argument== that modern immigration is about freedom: freedom to worship, freedom from oppression, freedom from want, freedom from fear, and freedom to create. Yes, immigrants have to overcome many problems. But according to Andrew Lam, a Vietnamese immigrant, "America remains the ideal that we all aspire to, everything you and I have ever dreamed of—transparency, opportunity, due process, fair play, and a promise of expansion and progress."

Talk About It Discuss the questions with a partner or in a small group. Do you think people born in the United States appreciate the hardships many immigrants face? Why or why not? Circle your opinion. Then, complete the sentence frame.

I think people born in the United States do/do not appreciate the

hardships because ______________________________________

____

____.

Important Words

fact: a statement that can be proven true

opinion: expresses a belief or a viewpoint that should be supported by facts or reason *(cognate: opinión)*

persuasive techniques: devices used to influence the audience in favor of the author's argument

Persuasive Techniques Writers often use persuasive techniques to convince their readers to agree with their opinions. To evaluate a writer's argument, you must determine what persuasive techniques are used, and whether they are supported by facts or opinions.

This chart shows a few examples of persuasive techniques.

Technique	Purpose	Example
1. Appeal to Authority	To call on the opinions of experts or other respected people	According to leading professors of economics, immigrants are an important part of the U.S. workforce.
2. Rhetorical Questions	To ask questions with obvious answers for effect	Isn't it our duty as Americans to protect and respect everyone?
3. Appeal to Emotions	To focus on a reader's fear, sympathy, pride, or other emotion	Keep America the "land of opportunity." Vote "yes" on this new law.

Talk About It Discuss the chart with a partner or in a group. What is the purpose of each technique? Do the examples match the description of each technique? Can you discuss other examples of each technique?

- -

Extend Language and Comprehension Read the passage. Then, use the chart to help you analyze the author's use of persuasive techniques.

It is important to remember that Americans are proud of their country. Don't we want a country that welcomes everyone? Shouldn't we believe in the values that made this country great? I believe that new immigrants represent the best of America. They work hard and are proud to be Americans. Isn't this the type of country we want?

Technique	
Purpose	
Effect	

Connect to Writing

Persuasive Paragraphs Think of all you have learned in this lesson. What new words did you use? How did you learn to identify persuasive techniques? Talk with a partner about what you learned.

On a separate sheet of paper, write two persuasive paragraphs that respond to the quote "America remains the ideal that we all aspire to." You can use information from the article, "The Newest Newcomers," or other resources.

Make sure to:

• take a clear position.

• use several persuasive techniques to support your position.

If you need help, circle your opinion. Then, complete the sentence frames.

Someone once said, "America remains the ideal that we all aspire to."

I believe this statement is/is not ________________________________

because ________________________________

________________________________.

According to ________________________________

________________________________.

Therefore, ________________________________

________________________________.

Writing Tips
Don't forget to

1. use persuasive words.

2. use facts and opinions.

3. revise your writing for appropriate word choice.

Connect to the Big Question 

Think about all the articles you read in this unit. What article did you like best? What article did you like the least? Then, think about your favorite article and tell what the article was about.

Now, take some time to share your final ideas. Answer this question: How does knowledge change our lives? Complete the sentence frame below.

Knowledge changes our lives by ________________________________

____

________________________________.

**Big Question Words
and Important Words**

adapt

argument

awareness

distinguish

empathy

enlighten

evolve

growth

history

ignorance

influence

insight

modified

process

question

reaction

reflect

represent

revise

statement

understanding

Vocabulary Review

Best Answer Read each question. Then, circle the best answer.

1. What is another word for "adapt"?
   A. change
   B. influence
   C. question
   D. reflect

2. Which is an example of "empathy"?
   A. a person who adapts to a new land
   B. a person who reflects on a serious problem
   C. a person who understands another person's feelings
   D. a person who challenges the truth

3. Which word refers to something that improves over time?
   A. understand
   B. question
   C. influence
   D. evolve

4. What does it mean to "reflect"?
   A. to challenge the truth of something
   B. to think calmly
   C. to have an effect on people
   D. to know something exists

5. If you "enlighten" people, you
   A. challenge them to prove the truth of something.
   B. have very little knowledge of their backgrounds.
   C. give them information to help them understand something.
   D. make arguments that modify or correct them.

Your Own Words Write a definition for these words.

1. insight ____

   ____.

2. history ____

   ____.

3. revise ____

   ____.

4. reaction ____

   ____.

5. understanding ____

   ____.

Main Idea The main idea of a text is the most important thing an author wants to say. Read the passage below. Then, fill in the chart.

Teens like to express themselves through clothing. Jeremy prefers wearing T-shirts and jeans to school. Sometimes he'll wear a baseball cap. Travis, on the other hand, likes to dress up. He often wears a tie and dress pants to school. It makes him feel more professional and "grown up."

Main Idea: ____

____

Supporting Detail: _______________________________________

Supporting Detail: _______________________________________

Is the Main Idea Stated or Implied? _______________________

Persuasive Appeals Some authors use persuasive appeals to convince the reader of their beliefs or opinions. Read the passage. Then, fill in the chart.

Schools are moving toward tighter dress codes, which will insure the safety of children across the nation. After strict dress codes were enacted, our school district reported a drop in the number of conflicts. According to one survey, 75% of teens agreed that safety was more important than personal style. Now, some people are arguing that dress codes violate a student's right to freedom of expression. But the welfare of children is more important than how they dress. Children should not be placed in an unsafe learning environment because some kids refuse to follow a dress code.

Claim: ____

Support:____

Persuasive Technique Used: _______________________________

What kind of knowledge changes our lives?

In this unit, I read:

In this unit, I:

- learned new vocabulary words.
- read about different topics.
- used supporting details.
- learned about implied details and stated details.
- used persuasive words.
- used persuasive techniques.
- learned about the main idea.
- learned about persuasive appeals.
- wrote a main idea outline.
- wrote a persuasive essay.
- wrote a main idea paragraph.
- wrote a descriptive essay.
- wrote persuasive paragraphs.

Reflection Think about what you learned in this unit. Complete each sentence frame. Share your answers with your teacher and classmates.

I wonder ____.

I learned ____.

I discovered ____.

I still want to know ____.

I still don't understand ____.

Does all communication serve a positive purpose?

In this unit, I will read:

In this unit, I will:

- learn new vocabulary words.
- read about different topics.
- pay attention to punctuation as I read.
- learn about reading rates.
- picture the action.
- analyze long sentences.
- learn about reading fluently.
- learn to paraphrase.
- write about how to read fluently.
- write a story.
- write about my reading rate.
- write a compare and contrast essay.
- write a simple paraphrase.
- write a biography.
- write a complex paraphrase.

Does all communication serve a positive purpose?

Connect to the Big Question

Answer these questions. Discuss your answers with your teacher and classmates.

> How do you know when communication is positive? How do you know when communication is negative?

Extend the Big Question

Read each sentence frame. Write your opinions in each blank.

> An example of positive communication is ___________
>
> ___________________________
>
> ___________________________
>
> ___________________________.
>
> I know it is positive when ______
>
> ___________________________
>
> ___________________________
>
> ___________________________.
>
> An example of negative communication is ___________
>
> ___________________________
>
> ___________________________
>
> ___________________________.

Discuss your opinions with your teacher and classmates.

Big Question Words

Use your definitions from page 34 of the *Review and Assess* book.

confusion
(cognate: confusión)

connection
(cognate: conexión)

context
(cognate: contexto)

convey

discourse
(cognate: discurso)

emotion
(cognate: emoción)

explanation
(cognate: explicación)

interact

isolation

language

meaning

misinterpret
(cognate: malinterpretar)

respond
(cognate: responder)

self-expression

verbal
(cognate: verbal)

Vocabulary Workshop

Examples and Non-examples Fill in an example and a non-example for each of the Big Question Words.

Big Question Word	Example	Non-example
confusion		
emotion		
verbal		
meaning		
self-expression		
language		
isolation		
context		

Sentence Frames Read each sentence frame. Think about the Big Question Word it contains. Then, complete each sentence.

1. The **connection** between _________________________

   was ____.

2. They **interact** via _________________________________

   ____.

3. Her smile and manner **convey** ___________________

   ____.

4. His **explanation** of _____________________________

   is ____.

5. Their **discourse** led us to believe they ___________

   ____.

Word Analysis

Suffixes A suffix is a letter or group of letters added to the end of a word. A suffix can change the spelling of a word and its part of speech, as well as its meaning.

For example, the word *explanation* contains the word *explain* and the suffix *-tion*. The word *explain* means "to make clear." The suffix *-tion* means "process" or "the act of." So, *explanation* means "the act, or process, of making clear." Also, notice how the spelling of the word changes when the suffix is added.

Some people use a letter as an explanation.

Make New Words Use the suffixes to make new words. Use a dictionary if you need help with spelling changes.

Word	Suffix	New Word
interpret	-tion	
mean	-ness	
art	-ist	
move	-ment	
emotion	-less	
context	-ual	
response	-ive	

Write Sentences Use five words from the chart to write five sentences.

____.

____.

____.

____.

____.

Lesson 1
Does all communication serve a positive purpose?

Vocabulary

Important Words

convey: to communicate something in words, pictures or other ways

emotion: a feeling, such as happiness, anger, or sadness
(cognate: emoción)

isolation: the act of being set apart from other people or a feeling of loneliness

pattern: a routine or set way of doing something
(cognate: patrón)

self-expression: the act of communicating to others your own feelings and personality

Concept Words

disgusting: very offensive or insulting

horror: a very deep fear
(cognate: horror)

special effects: sounds and other features that are used in movies
(cognate: efectos especiales)

Horror Movies

Dialogue

Two teens are talking about horror movies. Read the dialogue. Then, review the vocabulary words you read.

Teen 1: Do you want to see a movie after school? I was thinking of seeing something scary.

Teen 2: No thanks, I don't like movies to fill me with horror.

Teen 1: Are you kidding? Why not?

Teen 2: All the violence and gore is disgusting. Plus, the plot usually follows a predictable pattern. I think horror movies are boring. Why do you like them?

Teen 1: I like the special effects. They are so realistic. Plus, it's just plain fun getting scared. I can't believe you don't like any scary movies!

Teen 2: Well, I like movies with more of a story and drama behind the horror. Some older films show monsters that convey more emotion and self-expression. It's more interesting to watch these monsters because they make you think about their isolation and why they became monsters. It makes you think about yourself.

Teen 1: Now that sounds boring.

Teen 2: But why should violence be fun? It leaves nothing to the imagination.

Teen 1: Because it looks cool!

Talk About It Discuss the questions with a partner or in a group. Do you like horror movies? Why or why not? Circle your opinion. Then, complete the sentence frame.

I like/do not like horror movies because _________________

____

____.

Read the article. As you read, think about these questions:
- What makes horror movies scary?
- How have horror movies changed over the years?

Oooh, Scary!

Movies that fill viewers with **horror** have been around since 1896. They were black and white and silent. Then, in 1925, an actor by the name of Lon Chaney pioneered the use of make-up to make his characters look scary and **disgusting**. Chaney's famous appearance in *Phantom of the Opera* made audiences scream with fright.

Chaney's monsters, however, weren't just ugly. They were full characters whose minds were twisted by **isolation**, and filled with inner **emotions** of fear, anger, and pain. They usually didn't start out as evil monsters. Their behaviors were often the result of how society reacted to them. These monsters made audiences think about their own dark sides. The characters **conveyed** the message that all humans feel the need for **self-expression**, love, and understanding.

By contrast, today's monsters seem to have one purpose: to scare people. **Special effects** and advanced make-up techniques have surpassed anything Lon Chaney could have imagined. Some people claim that today's horror movies all follow the same **pattern** and rely solely on blood and gore for entertainment. They say that the blood and gore is the reason people go to horror movies—to be scared. Should we accept the horrible without looking for insights into what it means?

Older films relied more on acting than special effects to frighten audiences.

Talk About It Discuss the questions with a partner or in a group. Do you like the older style or the newer style of horror movies? Why? Circle your opinion. Then, complete the sentence frame.

I like/don't like _______________________________________

because _______________________________________

_______________________________________.

Important Words

pause: to stop reading aloud *(cognate: pausa)*

punctuation: the marks you see in sentences, like a period or a comma *(cognate: puntuación)*

read fluently: to read smoothly while also understanding the text and what the author is saying

Punctuation and Fluency Fluency is the ability to read easily and with expression and understanding. Punctuation can help you read fluently. End marks, commas, dashes, and semicolons help group words into complete thoughts and can tell you when to pause. Punctuation helps you become a fluent reader.

Punctuation	Type of Pause
period (.)	Complete stop.
colon (:)	Almost as strong as a period. Voice changed just enough so that a listener knows to expect more.
semicolon (;)	Not as strong as a colon. Pause briefly.
comma (,)	A slight pause.
exclamation point (!)	Complete stop, with more emphasis in voice to indicate strong emotions
question mark (?)	Complete stop, with voice changed to indicate a question.

Talk About It Work with a partner. Discuss each of the punctuation marks and what they represent. Use the article, "Oooh, Scary!" and practice reading some of the sentences.

Extend Language and Comprehension Read the dialogue below. Follow the steps in the chart.

Mark the Text
Circle punctuation marks.
Underline words that should be emphasized.
Bracket phrases or groups of words to read together.

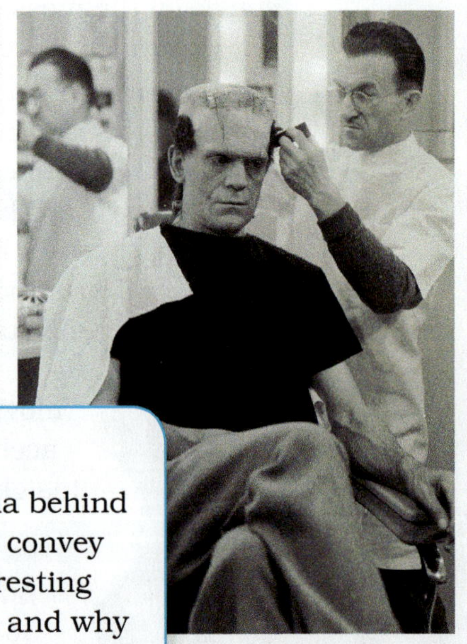

Teen 1: I can't believe you don't like any scary movies!

Teen 2: Well, I like movies with more of a story and drama behind the horror. Some older films show monsters that convey more emotion and self-expression. It's more interesting because it makes you think about their isolation and why they became monsters. It makes you think about yourself.

Teen 1: Now that sounds boring.

Teen 2: Why should blood and violence be fun? It leaves nothing to the imagination.

Teen 1: Because it looks cool!

Connect to Writing

How to Read Fluently Think of all you have learned in this lesson. What new words did you use? How did you learn to read fluently? Talk with a partner about what you learned.

On a separate sheet of paper, write instructions to a friend about how to read fluently. Make sure to include:

- tips for paying attention to punctuation

- tips on how to read aloud

If you need help, use the sentence frames.

When reading fluently, you first need to _______________________

____.

This will help you _____________________________________

____.

As you read, you should _______________________________.

This will help you _____________________________________

____.

Extension Activity Writing

Write a Story On separate sheet of paper or on a computer, write your own scary story. Are your characters angry for some reason? Are they afraid or in pain? Use details to describe your story.

Tips for Your Story

- Use vivid and fresh language; make strong comparisons.

- Be creative and artistic.

- Make use of your senses: describe the sights, smells, sounds, and textures.

- Describe your surroundings.

- Use the Writing Process Handbook at the end of this book. This will help you with prewriting, drafting, and revising. If you are writing on a computer, follow the directions for your word-processing program.

**Lesson 2
Does all communication serve a positive purpose?**

Vocabulary

Important Words

explanation: a statement that helps you understand a situation or an idea
(cognate: explicación)

interact: to talk, behave, or have some kind of exchange with people

respond: to react to someone or something by thinking, speaking, or taking action
(cognate: responder)

verbal: made up of words
(cognate: verbal)

Concept Words

advertising: the display of products on the radio, on television, in stores, or outside which makes people want to buy them

billboard: a large outdoor sign

distracting: disturbing or causing worry or alarm
(cognate: distracción)

Advertising

Dialogue

A teen and a parent are discussing outdoor advertisements. Read the dialogue. Then, review the vocabulary words you read.

Teen: Look at that cool billboard! I've never seen one with moving verbal messages and images before.

Parent: I can't look at it—I'm driving.

Teen: Wait, it's asking us to respond. I've never seen a billboard that interacts with drivers before! Now it's changing to a different message. That's really cool.

Parent: It's really distracting. I don't think that's a safe form of advertising. What if I ran off the road trying to read and respond to it? What kind of explanation would I give the police officer?

Teen: You could say you were reading an interactive billboard.

Parent: Roadside advertisements used to be smaller and safer. I remember when I was a kid the billboards used to entertain us with words. Now they use moving images.

Teen: I like the cool moving images.

Parent: As a passenger, you can appreciate them, but as a driver, it's another story. I wish I could drive without the constant interruptions! It would be nice just to enjoy the countryside for a change.

Talk About It Discuss the questions with a partner or in a group. What do you think of billboard advertisements? Are they entertaining or distracting? Circle your opinion. Then, complete the sentence frame.

I think billboard advertisements are /are not _______________

____

because ____

____.

Read the article. As you read, think about these questions:
- How do billboards affect drivers?
- How does the topic of the article relate to the topic of the dialogue?

As Big as All Outdoors

Do you read roadside **billboards**? Are they interesting or **distracting** to you? Roadside **advertising** has been popular since the 1920s. But have some billboards become roadside distractions today? Many concerned people believe they have and that these billboards are both annoying and dangerous.

Roadside billboards have been around since the 1920s.

In 1965, Congress was moved to **respond** to these concerns by passing the Highway Beautification Act. Unfortunately, the law was weak and billboards multiplied. This prompted some states, such as Maine, Vermont, Alaska, and Hawaii, to pass their own laws banning highway advertising. In other states, the number of billboards continues to grow. Many people worry that billboards are distracting drivers and putting them in danger.

What makes these billboards so distracting? One **explanation** is the use of digital billboards. Advertisers have known for some time that people are entertained and attracted to moving digital images. So they have created huge digital billboards to attract attention. For example, one advertiser in Las Vegas projected an image that was over 1,100 feet tall! Other billboards actually **interact** with drivers by presenting personalized **verbal** messages.

Some advertisers have published study results stating digital ads are not dangerous. Yet, doesn't common sense tell us that people should not be responding to personal messages while they are driving?

Talk About It Discuss the questions with a partner or in a group. Do you think roadside advertising should be allowed? Why or why not? Circle your opinion. Then, complete the sentence frame.

I think roadside advertising should/should not be allowed because

____

____ .

Important Words

adjust: to make changes as you do something *(cognate: ajustar)*

reading rate: your reading speed

Reading Rate Your reading rate is the speed at which you read a passage. Depending on your purpose for reading, you will want to adjust your reading rate to match your reading purpose. Adjusting your reading rate also helps reading fluency.

Ask yourself	Example answers
What kind of text is it?	Newspaper, book, magazine
Why am I reading it?	To write a report, for entertainment, to learn information, to complete a lesson
What reading rate should I choose?	Slow, fast, skimming, or a combination of different speeds

Example text	Purpose	Reading rate
Magazine article on a rock star	Entertainment	Read quickly to find interesting details
Biography of a famous leader	Research report	Read slowly, selecting facts for your report

Talk About It Work with a partner or in a small group. Discuss some of the examples from the chart. Why would you choose different reading rates for different types of text?

Extend Language and Comprehension When you read fluently, you read with understanding. Read the passage. Then, fill in the chart.

Each year, advertisers compete to create the largest, most technologically advanced outdoor advertisements. In 2007, a resort in Nevada featured a 250-foot ad, which was soon outdone by another advertisement in Las Vegas that was much taller. Advertisers are now using digital images that can change and move, show videos, and even interact with drivers.

Source	
Purpose	
Reading Rate	

Connect to Writing

My Reading Rate Think about all you have learned in this lesson. What new words did you use? How did you learn to set a reading rate to improve your reading fluency? Talk with a partner about what you learned.

On a separate sheet of paper, write a paragraph that answers the following questions:

- How did you decide your reading rate? Give an example.
- How did your reading rate help you to read more fluently?

If you need help, use the sentence frames.

I decided my reading rate by ________________________________

____.

For example, ____

____.

My reading rate helped me ________________________________

____.

Writing Tips
Don't forget to

1. think about how your purpose affects your reading rate.
2. think about how your reading rate helps you achieve fluency.
3. edit your writing for spelling.

Extension Activity   Writing

Write an Essay Write an essay comparing and contrasting two billboards that you find entertaining or distracting. Describe them both and discuss the similarities and differences between your two choices. Then, analyze the advantages and disadvantages of both.

Tips for Your Essay

- State your descriptions and opinions clearly.
- Use compare and contrast words.
- Organize your essay carefully.
- Use the Writing Process Handbook at the end of this book. This will help you with prewriting, drafting, and revising. If you are writing on a computer, follow the directions for your word-processing program.

Lesson 3
Does all communication serve a positive purpose?

Vocabulary

Important Words

connection: when people or groups relate on an emotional level
(cognate: conexión)

meaning: the purpose or intention of something
(cognate: confusión)

misinterpret: to be incorrect about the meaning of words or gestures
(cognate: malinterpretar)

possible: can be done or can happen
(cognate: posible)

respond: to react to someone or something by thinking, speaking, or taking action
(cognate: responder)

Concept Words

fame: the state of being widely honored and praised
(cognate: fama)

media: the various formats of mass communication, such as TV, radio, the Internet, and newspapers

overemphasis: too much importance on one thing

Sports and Fame

Dialogue

Two teens are discussing role models. Read the dialogue. Then, review the vocabulary words you read.

Teen 1: Who's your favorite basketball player?

Teen 2: Michael Jordan, without a doubt. I want to be like him someday.

Teen 1: Who doesn't? But really, his kind of fame only happens to a small number of kids.

Teen 2: You don't think it's possible for me?

Teen 1: Seriously? It's possible but not likely. The media makes kids think it's easy to become rich and famous—but it's not.

Teen 2: Why do you say that? I don't get your meaning.

Teen 1: Due to an overemphasis on professional sports in the news, lots of kids misinterpret the message. Some kids respond by dropping out of school because they think they don't need an education to become a professional athlete.

Teen 2: So what am I supposed to do?

Teen 1: Make a connection with other role models. Think about other careers. Who do you think is the most successful African American in America?

Teen 2: Oprah Winfrey.

Teen 1: She is among the top five, but the other four are business people. You see? The media doesn't tell you everything!

Talk About It Discuss the questions with a partner or in a group. Who is your role model? Why do you want to be like him or her?

My biggest role model is _______________________.

I want to be like him/her because _______________________

_______________________.

Read the article. As you read, think about these questions:
- How do young people choose role models?
- How does the topic of the article relate to the topic of the dialogue?

Do You Want to Be "Like Mike"?

Have you ever dreamed of becoming a professional athlete? Today, the chances of becoming the next Michael Jordan are one in ten thousand. Even though the chances are slim, millions of young high school students still feel it is possible to reach that level of fame. Many students respond to the media's overemphasis on athletes and entertainers. They make students believe that, if they want to be successful, they must become an athlete or entertainer.

African-American and Latino-American students are particularly open to making this connection. Most of the African-American and Latino people portrayed in the media are either athletes or entertainers. This leads students to misinterpret the meaning behind those images. They will assume that the careers they are most likely to succeed in are sports or entertainment, when the reality is African-Americans and Latinos succeed in all types of careers—all of which take hard work.

Many students think they have to abandon their studies to become a star in the sports or entertainment world. The truth is that you don't have to leave your education behind in order to follow your dreams. Just think of the football stars Emmit Smith and Ahmad Rashad: they went back to school. Michael Jordan finished his degree while he was playing. Now that's real star quality!

Medicine is one example of a successful career option.

Talk About It Discuss the questions with a partner or in a group. Think about your role models. Do they come from media or your community? Why do you admire them?

My role models mostly come from ___________________________.

I admire them because ___________________________

___________________________.

Important Words

clarify: to make clear
(cognate: *clarificar*)

paraphrase: to restate
in your own words
(cognate: *parafrasear*)

restate: to say in
another way

Picture the Action The text you read often contains details that describe the setting, characters, or actions in a story. Use these details to create a picture in your mind. This helps you clarify and restate what you are reading.

Read the passage below. Look for descriptive details.

Leo sat on the edge of the couch, his eyes wide with excitement as he watched his hero on TV, Antwan Jamison, run down the basketball court. Suddenly, Leo jumped up from the couch, yelling, "Yes!" He pumped his arms in the air while doing a small victory dance on the living room floor. His grandmother watched from the doorway, shaking her head.

Talk About It Work with a partner. What images or pictures do you get from the passage? Can you create a picture in your mind?

Extend Language and Comprehension When you paraphrase, you restate something in your own words. Read the passage. Form a clear picture in your mind of the descriptive details. Then, write a paraphrase of the passage. Use the chart to organize your thoughts.

Descriptive Details	What I Picture:	My Paraphrase
Jennifer tried to see Oprah Winfrey, but the crowd was pushing and shoving.		

Connect to Writing

Simple Paraphrase Think of all you have learned in this lesson. What new words did you use? How did you learn to use mental pictures to build understanding? How did you learn to paraphrase? Talk with a partner about what you learned.

On a separate sheet of paper, write a sentence from the article, "Do You Want to Be 'Like Mike'?" Then, paraphrase the sentence. Be sure to look for descriptive details that help you build understanding.

If you need help, use the sentence frames.

Sentence: ____

____

____

____.

This sentence is saying _________________________________

____

____

____.

Extension Activity   Writing

Write a Biography Write a biography about one of your role models. What are some of the things you admire and respect about this person? Look up some facts about his or her life. How did he or she become successful? Explain in detail to your readers why your role model is special.

Tips for Your Biography

- Be specific. Use concrete details to describe the person.

- If you need to do research, your teacher or librarian will be able to help guide you. Remember to cite both primary and secondary sources.

- Use the Writing Process Handbook at the end of this book. This will help you with prewriting, drafting, and revising. If you are writing on a computer, follow the directions for your word-processing program.

Lesson 4
Does all communication serve a positive purpose?

Vocabulary

Important Words

confusion: the act of being mixed up, unclear, or unsure about something *(cognate: confusión)*

continuum: a series of things that become different gradually *(cognate: continuo)*

frequently: happening often *(cognate: frecuentemente)*

language: the set of words a group of people uses to communicate with each other

Concept Words

abbreviation: a shortened form of a word or phrase, such as *Dr.* for *Doctor* or *Rd.* for *Road* *(cognate: abreviatura)*

harmful: capable of causing much damage

text message: a communication you send with a cell phone

Text Messaging

Dialogue

A teen and parent are discussing text messaging. Read the dialogue. Then, review the vocabulary words you read.

Parent: I'm concerned about how much time you spend sending **text messages**.

Teen: Why? What's wrong with it?

Parent: I think it can be **harmful** for a lot of reasons. The first of which is the cost. Do you realize how expensive it is?

Teen: No, but I know I use it **frequently**. If you want, I'll try to use it less often.

Parent: Yes, I'd like you to use it less. The second reason is all those **abbreviations** you use. I worry that it creates **confusion**. Also, I worry that you will lose your ability to write normally by using all of that shorthand **language**.

Teen: Oh please! It doesn't cause any confusion for me at all. I don't use those abbreviations when I write papers at school.

Parent: Which brings me to my biggest concern: your teacher informed me you have been text messaging during class. On the **continuum** of issues, this is the most serious. No wonder your grades have been suffering!

Teen: Class can be boring sometimes. So, I send text messages to my friends. Okay, if it bothers you so much I promise to pay attention in class and text less often.

Talk About It Discuss the questions with a partner or in a group. Do you or your friends use text messaging? Why do you think teens like it? Complete the sentence frame.

I think teens like text messaging because ______________________

____

____.

Read the article. As you read, think about these questions:

- What are the arguments against text messaging?
- How do supporters of text messaging respond?

Texting on Trial

Do you like to send text messages? Text messaging through cell phones is popular among teens, but it can be controversial among adults. People who think it's harmful have put texting on trial.

The first argument against text messaging is that the constant use of abbreviations takes away from a student's ability to write clear and well-organized papers. Supporters of texting say that language happens on a continuum, from very casual to very formal, and that it's unlikely that teens will confuse the two.

Opponents also argue that texting causes distractions and confusion in the classroom. Students are text messaging when they should be listening to their teachers. Supporters claim that the problem isn't text messaging. They claim that when kids get bored, they start sending messages. It's a problem teachers have to handle all the time.

People blame text messaging for a number of other problems as well. For example, some experts claim that teens who frequently stay up late texting do not get enough rest. Parents also complain about the high cost of text messaging. To both these complaints, supporters tell parents to set texting limits or take the phone away.

Text messaging is popular among teens.

Talk About It Discuss the questions with a partner or in a group. What is your verdict in the trial against texting? Is text messaging harmful for teens? Circle your opinion. Then, use the sentence frame.

I think text messaging is/is not harmful for teens because _________

____

____.

Important Words

analyze: to examine or to look at very closely (*cognate: analizar*)

paraphrase: to restate in your own words (*cognate: parafrasear*)

Analyze Long Sentences You can analyze long sentences by breaking them down into parts. This helps you understand and paraphrase what you are reading.

Identify the main actions and who or what performs them.	Daisy could not stay awake in class because she stayed up all night sending text messages to her friends.
Identify details that show when, where, how, or why each action is performed.	Daisy could not stay awake in class because she stayed up all night sending text messages to her friends.

Talk About It Discuss the chart with a partner or in a group. Why is it helpful to analyze long sentences? After you discuss your reasons, paraphrase the sentence in the chart.

Most schools do not allow texting in class.

Extend Language and Comprehension When you paraphrase, you restate something in your own words. Read and analyze the sentence below. Then, use the chart to organize your thoughts.

Sentence: After the phone bill reached over $100, Roger's mother began setting text messaging limits and threatened to confiscate the phone entirely.

Who performs the main actions in the sentence?	___________________________
What are the main actions in the sentence?	___________________________
When, where, how or **why** are the actions performed?	___________________________

Paraphrase: ___________________________

Connect to Writing

Complex Paraphrase Think of all you have learned in this lesson. What new words did you use? How did you learn to analyze long sentences and paraphrase? Talk with a partner about what you learned.

On a separate sheet of paper, write at least four sentences that paraphrase the article, "Texting on Trial." Focus on the following questions:

- What is the main idea of the article?

- What are two opposing viewpoints in the article?

If you need help, use the sentence frames.

The main idea of the article is ___________________________________

____ .

Some people argue ____

____

while others think that ____

____ .

Another concern is ____

____ .

Others say ____ .

Connect to the Big Question 

Think about all the articles you read in this unit. What article did you like best? What article did you not like? Then, think about your favorite article and say what the article was about.

Now, take some time to share your final ideas. Answer this question: Does all communication serve a positive purpose? Circle your opinion. Then, complete the sentence frame.

All communication does / does not serve a positive purpose because

____

____

____ .

**Big Question Words
and Important Words**

confusion

connection

context

continuum

convey

discourse

emotion

explanation

frequently

interact

isolation

language

meaning

misinterpret

pattern

possible

respond

self-expression

verbal

Vocabulary Review

Same Meaning Read the sentences. Fill in the blank with another word that has the same meaning as the underlined word.

1. In this context, I think we should consider our options carefully.

   In this _______________________, I think we should consider our options carefully.

2. The discourse over text messaging is heated.

   The _______________________ over text messaging is heated.

3. People express strong emotions about the issue.

   People express strong _______________________ about the issue.

4. Without her cell phone, she felt very isolated.

   Without her cell phone, she felt very _______________________.

5. He got angry because I didn't respond to his comment.

   He got angry because I didn't _______________________ to his comment.

Personal Response Complete each sentence with your response.

1. My family frequently _______________________

   _______________________.

2. Sometimes I misinterpret _______________________

   _______________________.

3. My _______________________

   _______________________ is a form of self-expression.

4. I have a great connection with _______________________

   _______________________.

5. I like to interact with _______________________

   _______________________.

Read Fluently Fluency is the ability to read easily and with expression and understanding. Choose one of the articles from the unit to read fluently. Then, use the chart to help determine your reading rate. Don't forget to pay attention to punctuation when you read.

Source	
Purpose	
Reading Rate	

Paraphrase When you paraphrase, you restate something in your own words. Read the sentence below. Then, fill in the chart.

Sentence: Text messaging can be dangerous for teens who aren't careful, particularly those who stay up late texting their friends.	
Who performs the main actions in the sentence?	__________________
What are the main actions in the sentence?	__________________
When, where, how or why are the actions performed?	__________________
Paraphrase: __________________	

 # Does all communication serve a positive purpose?

In this unit, I read:

In this unit, I:

- learned new vocabulary words.
- read about different topics.
- paid attention to punctuation as I read.
- learned about reading rates.
- pictured the action.
- analyzed long sentences.
- learned about reading fluently.
- learned to paraphrase.

- wrote about how to read fluently.
- wrote a story.
- wrote about my reading rate.
- wrote a compare and contrast essay.
- wrote a simple paraphrase.
- wrote a biography.
- wrote a complex paraphrase.

Reflection Think about what you learned in this unit. Complete each sentence frame. Share your answers with your teacher and classmates.

I wonder ____.

I learned ____.

I discovered ____.

I still want to know ____.

I still don't understand _____________________________________.

To what extent does experience determine what we perceive?

In this unit, I will read:

In this unit, I will:

- learn new vocabulary words.
- read about different topics.
- use important details.
- take notes.
- use compare and contrast words.
- use characteristics.
- learn to summarize.
- learn to compare and contrast.
- write a simple summary.
- conduct an interview.
- write a compare and contrast essay.
- write a complex summary.
- write compare and contrast paragraphs.
- write an autobiography.

To what extent does experience determine what we perceive?

Connect to the Big Question

Answer these questions. Discuss your answers with your teacher and classmates.

How do you know what you perceive is real? Why do people perceive things differently?

Extend the Big Question

Read each sentence frame. Write your opinions in each blank.

What I perceive is real to me

because _______________________

____

____

_______________________.

People perceive things differently

because _______________________

____

____

_______________________.

Personal experience impacts the

way we see _______________________

____

____

_______________________.

Discuss your opinions with your teacher and classmates.

Big Question Words

Use your definitions from page 45 of the *Review and Assess* book.

anticipate

background

bias

distortion

expectations

identity
(cognate: *identificar*)

impression
(cognate: *impresión*)

individual
(cognate: *individuo*)

insight

interpretation
(cognate: *interpretación*)

knowledge

manipulate
(cognate: *manipular*)

perspective
(cognate: *perspectiva*)

stereotype
(cognate: *estéreotipo*)

universal
(cognate: *universal*)

Vocabulary Workshop

Guess The Word Read each clue. Then fill in the line with the correct Big Question Word.

1. I am a single being, separate from a group.

   What word am I? _______________________

2. I expect or look forward to.

   What word am I? _______________________

3. I understand something by seeing its exact truth.

   What word am I? _______________________

4. I get people to do whatever I want.

   What word am I? _______________________

5. I am inclined to think something about someone before

   I know them. What word am I? _______________________

Complete the Chart Write a sentence using each Big Question Word listed.

Big Question Word	Sentence
identity	Her personal *identity* information was stolen after she used her credit card online.
stereotype	_______________________________________ _______________________________________.
knowledge	_______________________________________ _______________________________________.
universal	_______________________________________ _______________________________________.
background	_______________________________________ _______________________________________.

Word Analysis

Idioms An idiom is an expression that combines words to mean something different than what the words mean on their own. Idioms are common in English. You can look for clues to help you figure out the meaning. For example:

Idiom	He let the cat out of the bag.	Idiom	You're pulling my leg!
Meaning	He gave away the secret.	**Meaning**	You're joking!

Figure Out Meanings Read each idiom. Then, write what you think each idiom means.

Idiom	Meaning
Cat got your tongue?	
You knocked my socks off.	
She's just stringing him along.	

· ·

Words with Multiple Meanings Some words have more than one meaning. For example, the word *bright* is an adjective meaning "very smart." The word *bright* can also mean "filled with light." It is important to read the word in a sentence and look for context clues to help you determine the meaning.

For each word below, write two possible meanings. Use a dictionary if you need help.

cause	___________________________ ___________________________
question	___________________________ ___________________________
change	___________________________ ___________________________

Lesson 1
To what extent does experience determine what we perceive?

Vocabulary

Important Words

bias: an opinion that affects the way you present information

expectations: what you think or hope will happen in the future (*cognate: expectativas*)

perspective: your point of view, or the way you see and understand something (*cognate: perspectiva*)

universal: involving everyone in the world or in a specific group (*cognate: universal*)

Concept Words

demonstration: a public display of a group's feelings (*cognate: demostración*)

free speech: a natural right for U.S. citizens to speak, without restrictions or limits

protest: the act of disagreeing against something (*cognate: protesta*)

Protest

Dialogue

Two teens are talking about protests and free speech at their school. Read the dialogue. Then, review the vocabulary words you read.

Teen 1: Did you see the protest in front of the school?

Teen 2: No, what is it about?

Teen 1: It's a student demonstration protesting the decision to cut after school activities. There are a bunch of kids holding signs and chanting. They want all of us to walk out of our classes to support them.

Teen 2: Let's go!

Teen 1: Are you serious? My parents have high expectations for me. If they got called in to school because I was demonstrating, they'd ground me forever.

Teen 2: But this a demonstration about free speech!

Teen 1: Wait a minute. I thought you had a bias about not getting involved in anything political.

Teen 2: Hey, from my perspective, free speech is not just another political issue. This is America. The demonstrators have a right to express themselves. They are not hurting anyone.

Teen 1: What if the adminstration cracks down on demonstrations, and you get suspended?

Teen 2: I'll have to deal with it. Free speech is the right of all Americans. It is universal—and this includes teenagers.

Talk About It Discuss the questions with a partner or in a group. If there was a protest at your school would you walk out of class to support it? Why or why not? Circle your opinion. Then, complete the sentence frame.

If there was a protest at my school I would/would not walk

out of class to support it because ______________________

____.

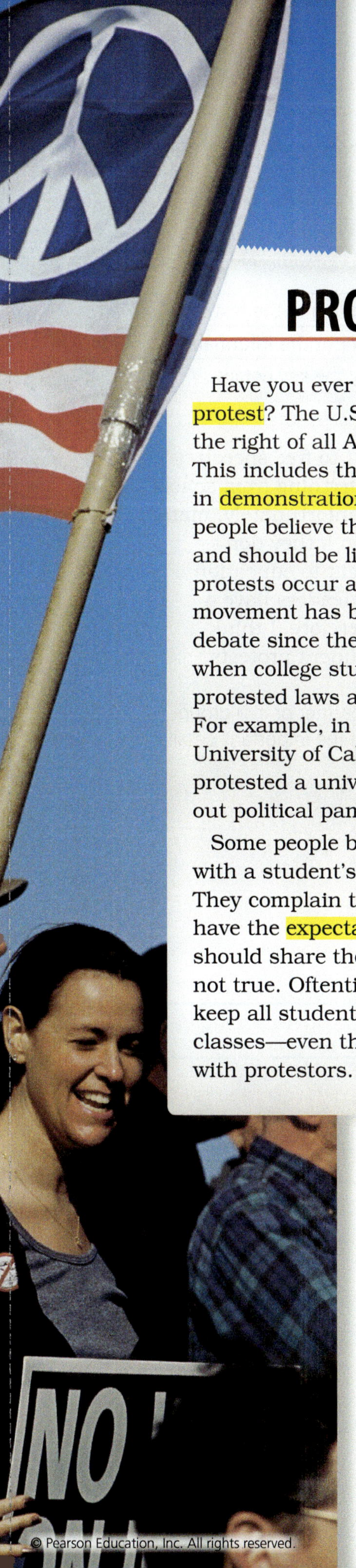

Read the article. As you read, think about these questions:

- What rights do students have to protest?
- How does the topic of the article relate to the topic of the dialogue?

PROS and CONS of PROTEST

Have you ever seen or been part of a **protest**? The U.S. Constitution protects the right of all Americans to **free speech**. This includes the right to participate in **demonstrations**. However, some people believe this right is not **universal** and should be limited when student protests occur at school. The free speech movement has been at the heart of this debate since the 1960s. This was a time when college students across the nation protested laws and government actions. For example, in 1964 students at the University of California at Berkeley protested a university ban on handing out political pamphlets.

Some people believe protests interfere with a student's right to an education. They complain that protesters seem to have the **expectation** that all students should share their **perspective**. This is not true. Oftentimes, demonstrations keep all students from going to classes—even those who disagree with protestors. In some cases, school

Students in the 1960s protested many different issues on college campuses.

officials have responded by calling police to come and control campus protests.

People who are against protests say that protestors interfere with the rights of others. Those who agree with protests say school officials show a **bias** against protests. From their perspective, schools have the responsibility to teach students about the democratic process, not punish them for exercising their rights.

Talk About It Discuss the questions with a partner or in a group. Do you think school officials have the right to limit protests? Why or why not? Circle your opinion. Then, complete the sentence frame.

I think school officials do/do not have the right to limit protests

because ____

____

____.

Important Words

important detail: a key piece of information (*cognate: detalle importante*)

main idea: the topic

summarize: to briefly state the most important events or ideas in a story or article

Important Details Important details are words or sentences that tell about the main idea. Identifying important details will help you summarize the text. When you summarize, you state the main idea and details in your own words.

To find important details

Ask, "Is this detail necessary for my understanding of the text?"

Ask, "Would the main idea hold together without this information?"

Pause sometimes while reading to restate only the key details.

Students and Protest

Students have been protesting the right to free speech since the 1960s. They have protested everything from school policy to government laws and actions. Unfortunately, many students feel pressure to participate, even if they don't support the protests. Students have a right to education and a safe learning environment. School leaders have a responsibility to protect all students. Therefore, I think schools should be stronger in limiting student protests.

Talk About It Discuss the questions with a partner or in a group. What is the main idea of the passage? How do the important details relate to the main idea?

Extend Language and Comprehension A summary is a short retelling of the main idea and details of the text. You can use a chart to help organize what you are reading. Use the article, "Pros and Cons of Protest," to complete the chart.

Title	Pros and Cons of Protest
Main Idea	
Important Detail	
Important Detail	
Important Detail	

Connect to Writing

Simple Summary Think about all you have learned in this lesson. What new words did you use? How did you learn to identify important details and create summaries? Talk with a partner about what you learned.

On a separate sheet of paper, write at least three sentences that summarize the article, "Pros and Cons of Protest."

If you need help, use the sentence frames.

The article, "Pros and Cons of Protest," is about _Possible response: student rights to free speech at school._

One argument against student protests is _that they disrupt the education of other students._

One argument in support is _that students are learning about democracy._

Extension Activity   Listening and Speaking

Conduct an Interview Conduct an interview about the restrictions on college students' rights to protest on campus. If you were a college student, what would you think? If you were a reporter, what would you ask the student? Work together to come up with a list of questions. Take turns playing the part of the reporter and the person being interviewed.

Tips for Your Interview

- Gather evidence on your topic.
- Stay focused. Try not to stray from your topic.
- If you are the person being interviewed, respond specifically to the questions you are asked.
- Gather and organize your questions and answers into a polished presentation.

To what extent does experience determine what we perceive?

Vocabulary

Important Words

appropriate: right or fitting for a situation *(cognate: apropriado)*

background: the culture and values with which a person has been raised

discipline: the ability to control your thoughts or behavior *(cognate: disciplina)*

identity: the set of characteristics that make you who you are *(cognate: identidad)*

stereotype: a belief about a group of people, based on knowing only a few *(cognate: estereotipo)*

Concept Words

besieged: to be surrounded by negative forces

monarch: another word for a king, queen, or royal leader *(cognate: monarca)*

royalty: having to do with nobility, such as kings and queens *(cognate: realeza)*

The Right to Privacy

Dialogue

Two teens are discussing royalty and the right to privacy. Read the dialogue. Then, review the vocabulary words you read.

Teen 1: Can you believe it? Prince Harry and his girlfriend went on another expensive vacation. I wish I was royalty! Imagine what your background would have been like if you had a monarch for a grandmother! You could do anything you want.

Teen 2: That's a stereotype about how the royal family lives. Maybe they're rich, but I think it would be terrible to be them. Imagine being besieged by photographers every day of your life. Papers would explore every little part of your personal life and identity.

Teen 1: Well, that's the price you pay for being famous. I think it's ok that the media cover their lives. The public has a right to know what they're doing.

Teen 2: Why? Do you think we have that right just because they are royalty?

Teen 1: Yes! The royals should show some discipline. They are supposed to be role models, but they often don't demonstrate appropriate behavior. The media lets us know exactly what they do in real life.

Teen 2: I bet you would change your mind if you were constantly in the public eye.

Talk About It Discuss the questions with a partner or in a group. Would you like to be part of a royal family? Why or why not? Circle your opinion. Then, complete the sentence frame.

I would/would not like to be part of a royal family because

____

____

____.

Read the article. As you read, think about these questions:
- Do royal famalies have the right to privacy?
- Does the public have the right to know about the private lives of royals?

Royal Right TO PRIVACY

Some blame the paparazzi for Princess Diana's death.

Have you ever wished you were part of a royal family? Depending on how much you value your privacy, you may want to think again. In the past, royalty were treated with more respect by the media and the public. Today, however, royalty are often besieged by journalists and photographers, called "paparazzi." These photographers exhibit little discipline and will chase their subject through the streets when trying to get a story.

In Great Britain, for example, the monarch and all the members of the family are treated like celebrities. True to the stereotype of a celebrity, Britain's royal family is wealthy and their background is well-known. One of the most famous members was Princess Diana. She was killed in a car accident in 1997 after trying to escape the paparazzi. Today, her sons, Prince Harry and Prince William, are constantly followed by photographers seeking gossip about their private lives. When the press learned the identity of the prince's girlfriend, paparazzi followed her home as well. In an attempt to help the press show appropriate behavior, the princes schedule regular press conferences to give the public information about their lives. In exchange, they expect the press to leave them alone. Some reporters respect this arrangement, while others continue to harass the royals. Do they have the right to privacy?

Talk About It Discuss the questions with a partner or in a group. Do Prince Harry and Prince William have the right to privacy? Why or why not? Circle your opinion. Then, complete the sentence frame.

I think they do/do not have the right to privacy because __________

____

____.

Important Words

element: another word for *detail* (cognate: *elemento*)

summarize: to briefly state the most important events or ideas in a story or article

Take Notes When you take notes, you write down the most important elements of what you read. For example, in informational articles, the elements you write down are the key details of the article. Using these details will help you summarize the text.

Talk About It Reread the article "Royal Rights to Privacy." Discuss with a partner or in a group. Identify some of the key details in the article. Why are these details important? Write at least four key details here.

Key Detail: _______________________________

____

Key Detail: _______________________________

____

Key Detail: _______________________________

____

Key Detail: _______________________________

____

Extend Language and Comprehension Use the details above to create a short summary of the passage.

____

____

____

____

____

____

Connect to Writing

Complex Summary Think about all you have learned in this lesson. What new words did you use? How did you learn to take notes and create summaries? Talk with a partner about what you learned.

On a separate sheet of paper, write a complex summary of the article, "Royal Charity."

Writing Tips
Don't forget to
1. look for main ideas.
2. identify key details.
3. use effective transitions.

Royal Charity

Being a member of the British Royal Family is not just about spending relaxing days in the palace being served by butlers. As representatives of the Queen, members have a duty to become active in the community. They join and sponsor charities, formal institutions, travel to foreign countries, and attend hundreds of public events every year.

Each member decides how they would like to distribute their time and wealth. Princess Diana was well known for her generous donations to many charities. Her sons Prince William and Harry continue to donate to their mother's favorite charities. They have their own personal favorites, too—Prince William recently helped launch a 5,000-mile bicycle ride across Africa to support the Tusk Trust, an organization that helps Africans build better lives in harmony with their environment.

Because of all of the time they spend in the public eye doing public service, members often draw a lot of media attention. Prince William's personal life, for example, is a frequent subject in the news. There's always a downside to a charmed life!

Extension Activity Writing

Write a Compare and Contrast Essay Write an essay comparing and contrasting royalty and celebrity. How are kings and queens and their families different from stereotypical celebrities? How are they similar? What are the advantages and disadvantages of belonging to either group?

Tips for Your Essay

- State your descriptions and opinions clearly.
- Use compare and contrast words.
- Organize your essay carefully.
- Use the Writing Process Handbook at the end of this book. This will help you with prewriting, drafting, and revising. If you are writing on a computer, follow the directions for your word-processing program.

Lesson 3

To what extent does experience determine what we perceive?

Vocabulary

Important Words

consider: to think carefully about something *(cognate: considerar)*

distortion: the act of changing the truth to give people a false idea

impression: a quick, general idea of someone or something *(cognate: impresión)*

individual: one person *(cognate: individuo)*

manipulate: to manage or control people unfairly *(cognate: manipular)*

Concept Words

clique: an exclusive group of people that may keep other people out of its group

humiliate: to make fun of someone *(cognate: humillar)*

superiority: the quality of feeling better or more important than others *(cognate: superioridad)*

Cliques

Dialogue

Two teens are discussing school cliques. Read the dialogue. Then, review the vocabulary words you read.

Teen 1: There go the popular girls. I wish they were my friends. Everyone likes them.

Teen 2: Not me. I'd rather be an **individual** than a member of a **clique**. Before joining any clique, **consider** the costs of being part of their group.

Teen 1: What do you mean? I always got the **impression** that they do what they want.

Teen 2: I think their leader does what she wants, but everyone else must follow her. Have you noticed how she **manipulates** the group? She has such an air of **superiority**.

Teen 1: No, what does she do?

Teen 2: She expects her followers to look, talk, dress, and act like her. If they don't, she **humiliates** them with gossip. I used to be friends with one of those girls. After she became part of that group, she turned into a bully. It was a complete **distortion** of her true personality. Is that what you want?

Teen 1: No, that's awful! Why would anyone want to be part of such an unhealthy friend group?

Teen 2: I think some of those kids are most comfortable being followers. Being in a clique tricks them into feeling like they are better than others.

Teen 1: Being in a clique is definitely not for me.

Talk About It Discuss the question with a partner or in a group. Have you ever wanted to be part of a clique? Why or why not? Circle your opinion. Then, complete the sentence frame.

I have/have not wanted to be part of a clique because

____

____

Read the article. As you read, think about these questions:
- What makes a friend group "healthy"?
- What makes a friend group "unhealthy"?

Many kids have friends through sports, clubs, and other activities.

In or Out of the In Crowd

Have you examined your group of friends lately? Experts encourage teens to consider whether the groups they belong to are healthy or unhealthy. Both types of groups may give individuals a sense of belonging, but at what cost? "Healthy" groups allow members to be themselves and to freely move in and out of the group. By contrast, an "unhealthy" group puts pressure on members to follow certain rules. This kind of group is called a clique.

Unlike "healthy" groups of friends, cliques usually have a very strong leader. The leader manipulates the followers into looking, acting, and dressing according to clique rules. If members stray from the leader's control, the leader may humiliate or threaten them. Cliques are also different from other groups in another way. Clique members convince themselves of their own superiority. They feed on distortion and cruel behavior to give the impression that they feel self-confident. Yet, experts agree that those teenagers who are truly self-confident see cliques as a waste of time.

It takes a lot of courage to leave a clique. However, once a member does leave, he or she often feels more confident and much better about himself or herself.

Talk About It Discuss the questions with a partner or in a group. How would you describe your group of friends? Is it healthy or unhealthy? Why? Use the sentence frame.

My friend group is _______________________________________

because _______________________________________

_______________________________________.

Important Words

alike: the same

compare: to show how things are alike or similar *(cognate: comparar)*

contrast: to show how things are different *(cognate: contrastar)*

different: not the same *(cognate: diferente)*

similar: the same *(cognate: similar)*

Compare and Contrast Words For the article you just read, your goal was to compare and contrast different types of groups of friends.

| When you show how two things are similar or alike, you compare them. | When you show how two things are different, you contrast them. |

This chart shows some words you can use to compare and contrast things.

Comparing Words	Contrasting Words
both	different from
same as	on the other hand
similar	by contrast
just like	as opposed to
likewise	unlike
as well as	however

Talk About It Discuss the chart with a partner or in a group. Circle the words that appear in the article, "In or Out of the In Crowd." Discuss why the words are comparing words or contrasting words.

Extend Language and Comprehension You can organize information to help clarify what you are reading. A Venn diagram can help you compare and contrast information. Use the article, "In or Out of the In Crowd," to compare and contrast members of "healthy" groups of friends with members of "unhealthy" cliques.

Members of "Healthy" Groups of Friends　　**Members of "Unhealthy" Cliques**

Differences　　Similarities　　Differences

Connect to Writing

Compare and Contrast Paragraph Think of all you have learned in this lesson. What new words did you use? How did you compare and contrast details from the article? Talk with a partner about what you learned.

On a separate sheet of paper, write a compare and contrast paragraph that answers the following questions:

- What similarities do all groups of friends share?

- How are cliques different from "healthy" groups of friends?

If you need help, use the sentence frames.

All groups of friends ___________________________________

___________________________ and ___________________________.

However, cliques are different because ___________________________

____.

By contrast, a "healthy" group of friends ___________________________

____.

Extension Activity   Writing

Write an Autobiography On separate paper or on a computer, write an autobiography about your life with your friends. Do you think your group of friends is "healthy"? What makes your group of friends special or unique?

Tips for Your Essay

- Apply your background knowledge in order to come up with specific and actual details and events. Your personal experiences are unique!

- Establish your main idea and use concrete examples and details to define and support it.

- Stay focused and maintain your concentration.

- Use the Writing Process Handbook at the end of this book. This will help you with prewriting, drafting, and revising. If you are writing on a computer, follow the directions for your word-processing program.

Vocabulary

Important Words

anticipate: to look forward to, expect, or make plans for something

constant: staying the same, happening over and over, or always there *(cognate: constante)*

interpretation: the meaning you find in events, pictures, or words *(cognate: interpretación)*

knowledge: Information acquired from study or through experience

presume: to believe something is true without getting proof *(cognate: presumir)*

Concept Words

collision: a violent crash or accident *(cognate: colisión)*

scandal: an outrage or a disgraceful event *(cognate: escándalo)*

warning: a message informing of danger

Preventing Tragedies

Dialogue

A teacher and student are discussing how to prevent tragedies. Read the dialogue. Then, review the vocabulary words you read.

Teacher: Today we are talking about preventing tragedies. Who can give me an example of a tragedy that could have been prevented?

Student: The sinking of the *Titanic*.

Teacher: Excellent example. Can someone tell us what caused the *Titanic* to sink?

Student: It had a collision with an iceberg.

Teacher: How do you think it could have been prevented?

Student: Many iceberg warnings were sent from other ships in the area. The captain should have been able to anticipate problems.

Teacher: As the captain, he had a lot of knowledge. Why did he ignore the warnings?

Student: He was overconfident because everyone came to presume the *Titanic* was unsinkable.

Teacher: Yes, and the scandal extended beyond the captain. There are many interpretations of the accident and who was to blame, but overconfidence is a constant theme. How does overconfidence lead to tragedies?

Student: It makes people feel invincible, and then, pay less attention to warning signs.

Talk About It Discuss the questions with a partner or in a group. Have you ever felt overconfident about something? How can overconfidence can cause unfortunate results?

An example of overconfidence is _______________________________

____.

This could cause ____

____.

Read the article. As you read, think about these questions:
- How could the tragedy have been prevented?
- Who do you think was responsible?

❧ THE TITANIC TRAGEDY ☙

In April 1912, the largest and most luxurious ship in the world, the *Titanic*, hit an iceberg and sank in the Atlantic Ocean. More than 1,500 people were killed. Many presumed that the *Titanic* was unsinkable. The fact that it sank made the tragedy even more of a scandal. Today, people still disagree over who was to blame.

The highly confident Captain Smith possessed a lot of knowledge about the northern Atlantic. He decided to take the shorter route across, despite receiving constant warnings of icebergs in the area. Since he didn't anticipate any problems, Captain Smith decided he didn't need to reduce the ship's speed. But the ship hit the iceberg. After the collision, the captain inspected the ship and realized it would sink. The crew quickly began evacuating passengers.

Unfortunately, the shipping company that built the *Titanic* did not prepare the ship for emergencies. Assuming the ship was unsinkable, the company did not equip the *Titanic* with enough lifeboats or properly train the crew for emergencies.

The *Titanic* tragedy still captivates people all over the world.

In addition, the crew didn't even have binoculars in the lookout tower. After the *Titanic* started to sink, the crew made many mistakes. They lit flares incorrectly and let lifeboats leave without being full. Some crew members prevented poorer passengers from getting into lifeboats, and others refused to help drowning victims. Ultimately, whoever you think is most to blame depends upon your interpretation of the events.

Talk About It Discuss the question with a partner or in a group. Who do you think was most responsible for the sinking? Why? Complete the sentence frame.

I think ________________________________ was most responsible

because ____

____

____ .

Important Words

characteristic:
something that is unique to
a specific thing or person
(cognate: característica)

compare: to show how
things are alike or similar
(cognate: comparar)

contrast: to show
how things are different
(cognate: contrastar)

Characteristics Characteristics are traits that describe people, characters, or details in the text. Identifying and interpreting characteristics can help you compare and contrast different people or things.

Characteristics of Captain Smith's overconfidence
He had a lot of knowledge of the north Atlantic.
He believed the ship was unsinkable.
He did not anticipate problems.

Talk About It Discuss with a partner or in a group. Find two more characteristics of overconfidence from the article, "The *Titanic* Tragedy." Use your background knowledge to interpret different people's actions. Complete the sentence frames.

_________________________________ showed overconfidence by

____.

_________________________________ showed overconfidence by

____.

. . . .

Extend Language and Comprehension You can organize information to help clarify what you are reading. Compare and contrast the characteristics of Captain Smith and the wealthy passengers on the *Titanic*. Use your background knowledge and information from the article, "The *Titanic* Tragedy," to fill in the chart.

People	Captain Smith	Wealthy passengers
Characteristic 1	_______________________	_______________________
Characteristic 2	_______________________	_______________________
Characteristic 3	_______________________	_______________________

Connect to Writing

Compare and Contrast Paragraphs Think of all you have learned in this lesson. What new words did you use? How did you compare and contrast characteristics? Talk with a partner about what you learned.

On a separate sheet of paper, write two compare and contrast paragraphs that answer the following questions

- How were people's responses to the sinking similar?
- How were people's responses to the sinking different?

If you need help, use the sentence frames.

> In comparing the responses of ________________________________
>
> and ________________________, they were similar because both
>
> ____.
>
> However, ____________________________ was different because
>
> ____,
>
> while ____________________ was ____________________
>
> ____.

Connect to the Big Question 

Think about all the articles you read in this unit. What article did you like best? What article did you not like? Then, think about your favorite article and say what the article was about.

Now, take some time to share your final ideas. Answer this question: How does our perception change as we gain more experience? Complete the sentence frame below.

> Our perception changes as we gain more experience by ____________
>
> ____
>
> ____
>
> ____
>
> ____.

To what extent does experience determine what we perceive?

Big Question Words and Important Words

- anticipate
- appropriate
- background
- bias
- consider
- constant
- discipline
- distortion
- expectations
- identity
- impression
- individual
- interpretation
- knowledge
- manipulate
- perspective
- presume
- stereotype
- universal

Vocabulary Review

Best Answer Read each question. Then, circle the best answer.

1. You should use "individual" to describe
   A. a group of people.
   B. one person.
   C. an organization.
   D. a couple.

2. Which word means "point of view?"
   A. background
   B. presume
   C. knowledge
   D. perspective

3. When you make plans for something, you
   A. anticipate it.
   B. interpret it.
   C. distort it.
   D. manipulate it.

4. A "stereotype" is
   A. a deep understanding of a group.
   B. the set of characteristics that define you.
   C. a belief about a group based on knowledge of a few.
   D. your education and other experiences.

5. What does it mean to "manipulate" people?
   A. to expect things from them
   B. to manage or control them unfairly
   C. to understand the way they think
   D. to have a false idea about them

Write Sentences Write a sentence for each word.

1. appropriate ____
   ____.

2. bias ____
   ____.

3. expectations ____
   ____.

4. identity ____
   ____.

5. consider ____
   ____.

Summarize When you summarize, you state the main idea and details of a story or article in your own words. Read the passage below. Next, fill in the chart to help organize what you have read. Then, write a summary of the passage on another sheet of paper.

Students should have the right to participate in protests and demonstrations at school. These demonstrations are an important part of a working democracy and are protected by the First Amendment to the U.S. Constitution. When schools limit these rights, they are sending students the wrong message. Some schools even ban protests altogether. If students promise not to behave irresponsibly, they should be able to speak their minds.

Main Idea	
Important Detail	
Important Detail	
Important Detail	

Compare and Contrast When you compare and contrast, you find similarities and differences between two things. Read the passage. Then, fill in the diagram to compare and contrast.

Marie has many groups of friends. She spends time with her friends from the soccer team, as well as a group of girls who are known as the "popular" clique in school. Her soccer friends are easy-going and usually get together to eat pizza after practice. By contrast, the "popular" girls usually sit together at lunch, gossiping and trying to act cool. Marie has noticed recently that she feels more comfortable with her soccer friends than with the other clique, but she likes individual friends from both groups.

Soccer Friends   **"Popular" Clique**

Differences   Similarities   Differences

To what extent does experience determine what we perceive?

In this unit, I read:

In this unit, I:

- learned new vocabulary words.
- read about different topics.
- used important details.
- took notes.
- used compare and contrast words.
- used characteristics.
- learned to summarize.

- learned to compare and contrast.
- wrote a simple summary.
- conducted an interview.
- wrote a compare and contrast essay.
- wrote a complex summary.
- wrote compare and contrast paragraphs.
- wrote an autobiography.

Reflection Think about what you learned in this unit. Complete each sentence frame. Share your answers with your teacher and classmates.

I wonder ____.

I learned ____.

I discovered ____.

I still want to know ____.

I still don't understand ____.

Can anyone be a hero?

In this unit, I will read:

In this unit, I will:

- learn new vocabulary words.
- read about different topics.
- identify cultural context.
- use my background knowledge.
- learn about worldviews.
- learn about cultural context.
- compare and contrast worldviews.
- write about cultural context.
- conduct a debate.
- write about background knowledge.
- tell a story.
- write about worldviews.
- write a descriptive essay.

Can anyone be a hero?

Connect to the Big Question

Answer these questions. Discuss your answers with your teacher and classmates.

What qualities do heroes possess? Would you like to be a hero?

Extend the Big Question

Read each sentence frame. Circle your opinion and write your opinions in each blank.

Heroes must be ______________
____
____
_________________________.

My heroes are ______________
____
____
_________________________.

I would / would not like be a

hero because ______________
____
____
____
_________________________.

Discuss your opinions with your teacher and classmates.

Big Question Words

Use your definitions from page 56 of the *Review and Assess* book.

attributes
(cognate: atributos)

character
(cognate: carácter)

conduct
(cognate: conducir)

courage
(cognate: coraje)

determination
(cognate: determinación)

honor
(cognate: honor)

inherent
(cognate: inherente)

integrity
(cognate: integridad)

legendary
(cognate: legendario)

persevere
(cognate: perseverar)

principles
(cognate: principios)

resolute
(cognate: resuelto)

responsibility
(cognate: responsabilidad)

sacrifice
(cognate: sacrificio)

selflessness

Vocabulary Workshop

Answer the Questions Read each question. Then, write the Big Question Word that best answers each question.

1. What word means the opposite of "quit"?
   ____

2. What word means the opposite of "cowardice"?
   ____

3. What word means to give something up for something greater? ______________________

4. What word means the opposite of "unknown"?
   ____

5. What word means almost the same as "obligation"?
   ____

Personal Response Read each sentence. Then, complete the sentence frames.

1. I learned the meaning of **integrity** from ______________
   ______________________________________.

2. The **attributes** of which I am least proud are __________
   ______________ because ______________
   ______________________.

3. I was **resolute** when ______________________
   ______________________.

4. The **principles** by which I live my life are ______________
   ______________ because ______________
   ______________________.

5. My **character** can best be described as ______________
   ______________________.

Context Clues Context clues can help you determine the meanings of unfamiliar words. Context clues can take different forms, such as examples, definitions, synonyms, and antonyms.

For instance, in the following sentence, the author uses an example as a context clue. Here the example is an act that illustrates the meaning of "selflessness."

Alejandro performed an act of *selflessness* when he volunteered to rebuild homes destroyed by the hurricane.

Search for Clues Circle the context clues in the following sentences. Then, write the type of clue it is.

1. My uncle's ability to paint is inherent, or deep-rooted.

   Type: ____

2. For the game's new design, he changed all the standards, which were measurements and benchmarks, that were old.

   Type: ____

Identify the Context Clues Read the sentences below. Circle the Big Question Word and underline the descriptive phrase that applies to that word. Then, label each phrase as *synonym*, *antonym*, or *definition*.

1. The candidate used all her determination to get reelected; she was purposeful and resolved about winning more votes than anyone else.

2. He enlisted in the military with a great deal of honor and optimism, but he ended up having to leave in disgrace.

3. As an actress, she was legendary because she was known for playing heroic and famous roles.

4. They took full responsibility for their company's actions, and they let the public know they would be liable and accountable for damages.

Lesson 1
Can anyone be a hero?

Vocabulary

Important Words

attributes: the qualities or characteristics of a particular person, place, or thing *(cognate: atributos)*

conceive: to think or imagine something *(cognate: concebir)*

determination: the strong desire and drive to reach a goal *(cognate: determinación)*

responsibility: something that you really have to do; your job *(cognate: responsabilidad)*

Concept Words

artificial intelligence: a type of science that tries to simulate human intelligence *(cognate: inteligencia artificial)*

breakthrough: an important discovery or invention

science fiction: a type of fiction that uses science concepts to tell stories *(cognate: ciencia ficción)*

Science and Responsibility

Dialogue

Two teens are discussing science and responsibility. Read the dialogue. Then, review the vocabulary words you read.

Teen 1: I wish I had a robot to do my homework. I'd have more time to have fun.

Teen 2: You've been reading too much science fiction.

Teen 1: Maybe, but artificial intelligence isn't that far off. I saw a video of a professor who conceived of and made a robot with human attributes. He wanted the robot to replace him in the office. I think with a little determination, scientists could make a robot that does high school homework!

Teen 2: What if the robot became aware of what you were doing and decided to give you F's to teach you a lesson? Scientists have a responsibility to think about the good and the bad effects that their inventions could have on people and the environment before creating such advanced machines.

Teen 1: You worry too much. Every scientific breakthrough leads to greater and better things.

Teen 2: I don't agree. Inventions are not all perfect, and we need to understand that.

Talk About It Discuss the question with a partner or in a group. Do you think scientific inventions help or hurt people? Circle your opinion. Then, complete the sentence frame.

I think scientific inventions help/hurt people because ________

____

____

____.

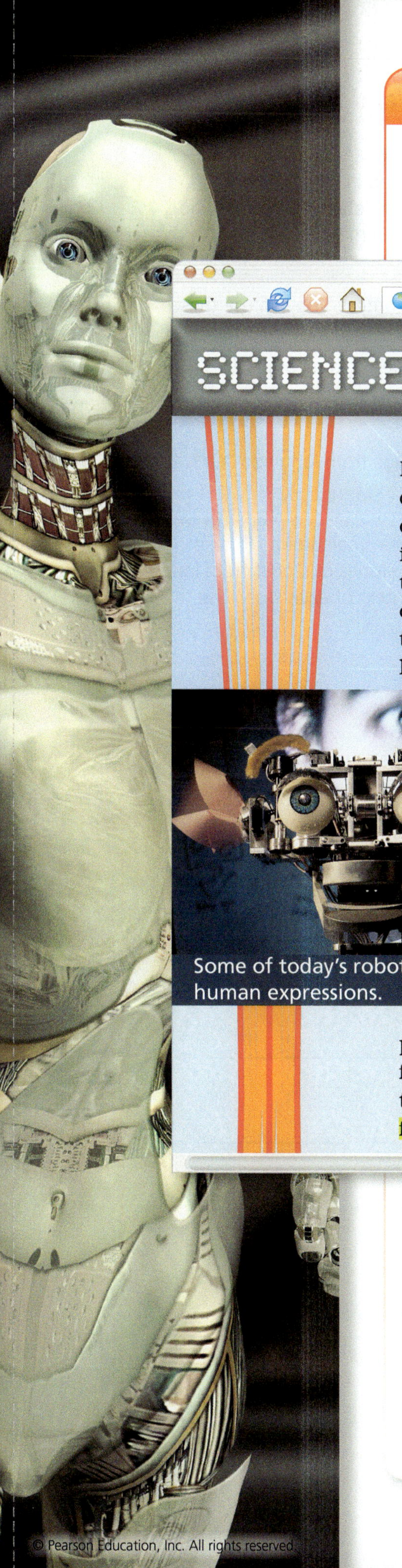

Read the article. As you read, think about these questions:
- Why is there a debate about scientific inventions?
- How does the topic of the article relate to the topic of the dialogue?

SCIENCE'S DOUBLE-EDGED SWORDS

On July 16, 1945, scientists tested the first atomic bomb. It was an incredible scientific **breakthrough** that led to the development of nuclear energy. However, the scientists who developed the bomb felt a tremendous **responsibility**. After seeing its destructive power, they found it difficult to **conceive** of using the bomb on human targets. However, President Truman felt differently. In his **determination** to end World War II, he decided to drop nuclear bombs on the cities of Hiroshima and Nagasaki, killing over 100,000 people.

Nuclear bombs, as well as other scientific discoveries, have led people to debate how scientific research can be a double-edged sword, or an issue that can have favorable *and* unfavorable consequences. While the discoveries benefit people, they may also create serious problems. The value of **artificial intelligence**, for example, is part of this debate.

Some of today's robots can make human expressions.

Robots are no longer the quirky, bleeping metal boxes of the past. Scientists have developed new robots with human **attributes**. They can imitate human expressions and perform basic tasks. While some people are excited about the future possibilities, others ask, "What if robots learn to teach themselves?" Angry robots have been the subject of **science fiction** for years. Could that become reality?

Talk About It Discuss the questions with a partner or in a group. Do you think there are drawbacks to artificial intelligence? Why or why not? Circle your answer. Then, complete the sentence frame.

I do/do not think there are drawbacks to artificial intelligence

because ____

____.

Important Words

context: surrounding text or information *(cognate: contexto)*

cultural: something related to everyday life that is shared by people in a given place or time *(cognate: cultural)*

historical: having to do with history *(cognate: histórico)*

Identify Cultural and Historical Context Cultural and historical context is related to the time period in which a piece of writing is set, or when it was written. These details include specific events, beliefs, and customs that reflect the time and culture of the work.

When you identify cultural and historical context, you can use these questions to help you:

- Does the piece of writing talk about a specific time or place?
- Does the piece of writing include beliefs or customs that reflect a specific culture?
- Does the piece of writing include language from long ago? Or is the language more modern?

Talk About It Work with a partner or in a small group. Think of your favorite stories. They can be modern stories or stories from long ago. Discuss the historical and cultural context of each story. Use the questions on this page to help you.

Extend Language and Comprehension Look for cultural and historical context in the article, "Science's Double-Edged Swords." Remember, the context can be the details in which a piece of writing is set, or in which it was written. Fill in the chart.

Cultural and historical context	Examples from the text
time and place	
events	
beliefs and customs	
language	

Connect to Writing

Use Cultural and Historical Context Think of all you have learned in this lesson. What new words did you use? How did you learn to identify cultural and historical context? Talk with a partner about what you learned.

Imagine you are giving instructions to a friend about how to find cultural and historical context. On a separate sheet of paper, answer the following questions:

- What is cultural and historical context?

- How do you find it in the text?

If you need help, use the sentence frames.

Cultural and historical context is _______________________________

____ .

You find it by ____ and

____ .

Writing Tips
Don't forget to

1. think about how to identify cultural and historical context.

2. use new vocabulary words.

3. create a chart to organize your ideas.

Extension Activity Listening and Speaking

Conduct a Debate Discuss with some of your classmates the positive and negative aspects of scientific advancement. Does every scientific breakthrough lead to greater and better things? Or, are there drawbacks? Consider the evidence and decide what you think. Then, divide into teams and debate your opinions with your classmates.

Tips for Your Debate

- State your opinions in a clear way; try to choose the right word.

- Use facts and examples to support your opinions.

- Consider the best way to convince your opponents. How would you win them over to your side? With logic? With emotion?

- Be prepared for your opponent's arguments and have counter-arguments ready.

- Remember to keep a cool head in your debate.

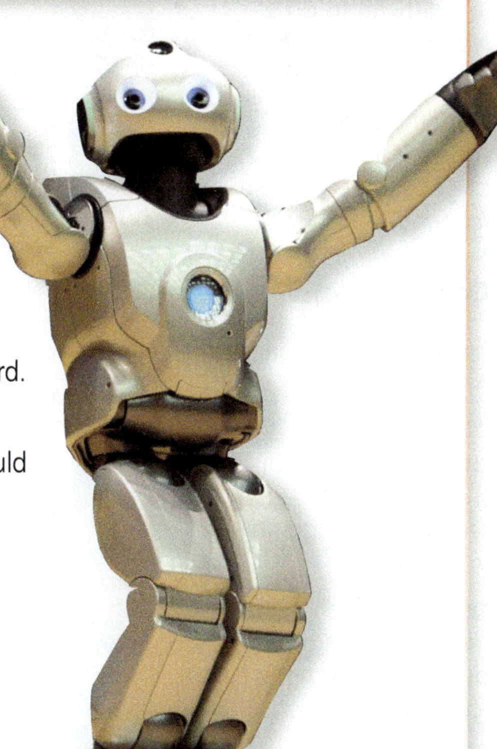

Lesson 2
Can anyone be a hero?

Vocabulary

Important Words

consult: to look for information from resources or people *(cognate: consultar)*

courage: the mental strength to face a difficult or dangerous situation *(cognate: coraje)*

irony: the difference between what is expected to happen and what actually happens *(cognate: ironía)*

persevere: to continue to do something or believe something, even when it is difficult to do so *(cognate: perseverar)*

sacrifice: to give up something in order to help someone else or get something else *(cognate: sacrificar)*

Concept Words

heroism: the qualities of being a hero *(cognate: heroísmo)*

oral history: a history that is collected and recorded through an interview

tradition: an important belief or custom passed down through time *(cognate: tradición)*

Oral Histories and Traditions

Dialogue

Two teens are discussing oral histories and traditions. Read the dialogue. Then, review the vocabulary words you read.

Teen 1: What are you doing for your report on culture and traditions?

Teen 2: I'm looking at the oral history of people who survived the Carlisle Indian boarding schools.

Teen 1: What do you mean "survived"? I thought those schools just taught Native American children how to live in a new culture.

Teen 2: Yes, they did, but the schools also required the children to sacrifice their own traditions. After consulting oral histories recorded from different tribes, I was inspired by the children's courage and ability to persevere. Did you know they couldn't wear their own clothes or speak their own languages? Imagine being taken from your family and forced into a school that was completely foreign. Their survival was a great act of heroism.

Teen 1: I'm doing my report on oral histories of Navajo heroes during World War II. Considering what you said, the irony is that the government's boarding schools wanted to erase Native American languages, but years later they relied on the Navajo language to help win the war.

Talk About It Discuss the question with a partner or in a group. Why are oral histories valuable? Use the sentence frame.

Oral histories are valuable because ________________________

____

____.

Read the article. As you read, think about these questions:
- How have cultural beliefs in the United States changed?
- How does the topic of the article relate to the topic of the dialogue?

The Youngest Heroes

In 1879, the U.S. government began running special "Indian" boarding schools that were designed to help Native American children fit in with "white" society. Many people believed these children had to **sacrifice** their **traditions** and culture in order to become "civilized."

From 1879 until the mid-1930s, Native American children were sent or were taken by force to these boarding schools. Upon arriving, the children were forced to cut their hair and dress differently. They were not allowed to speak their own languages. The **irony** is that during World War II, the U.S. government relied on the Navajo language to send important messages to help win the war.

In recent years, people have been able to **consult** those who survived the boarding schools and record their stories of **courage** and how they **persevered**. K. Tsianina Lomawaima recorded hours of memories from her father and other students of the Chilocco Indian School in Oklahoma. Likewise, Brenda Child did the same with the Minnesota Ojibwe. Thanks to each **oral history**, we now know about the **heroism** of a people who might otherwise be forgotten by time.

Talk About It Discuss the questions with a partner or in a group. Do you think cultural beliefs toward Native Americans have changed in the United States? Why or why not? Circle your answer. Then, complete the sentence frame.

I think cultural beliefs toward Native Americans have/have not

changed because ____

____.

Important Words

background: a person's experience or knowledge; the culture and values with which a person has been raised

cultural: something related to everyday life that is shared by people in a given place or time (*cognate: cultural*)

historical: having to do with history (*cognate: histórico*)

Background Knowledge Background knowledge is something that you already know about the topic you are reading. Background knowledge can also help you understand the cultural and historical context of a piece of writing.

Read the passage below. As you read, think about these questions:

Background Knowledge	
What ideas do I bring to this piece of writing?	What has happened to me, or what feelings have I had, that relate to this piece of writing?

Zitkala-Sa was a small child when she was taken to a Carlisle Indian boarding school. Everything was foreign to her, from the giant buildings to the strange staircases. "My body trembled more from fear than from the snow I trod upon," she said years later

Talk About It Discuss the questions with a partner or in a group. Using your background knowledge, discuss the historical and cultural context of the passage. What do the details tell you about Zitkala-Sa, her culture, and the time and place of the story?

Extend Language and Comprehension Reread the article, "The Youngest Heroes." Use your background knowledge to identify and analyze the cultural and historical context of the text. Then, fill in the chart.

Cultural and Historical Context from Text	Background Knowledge	Analysis

Writing Tips
Don't forget to

1. use your background knowledge of the topic.

2. identify cultural and historical details in the text.

3. use effective transitions.

Use Background Knowledge Think of all you have learned in this lesson. What new words did you use? How did you use background knowledge to analyze cultural and historical context? Talk with a partner about what you learned.

On a separate sheet of paper, write the answers to the following questions:

- What background knowledge did you use to understand the article, "The Youngest Heroes"?

- What cultural and historical context did you identify?

If you need help, use the sentence frames.

My background knowledge comes from _______________________

____

____.

The cultural and historical context of the article is _______________

____.

Extension Activity   Listening and Speaking

Tell Your Own Oral History Work with a partner. Each partner tells a story about him or herself: something specific that happened at home, in the neighborhood, at school, or at a relative's home. Try to recall all the details. Practice telling the story to your partner. Then, present it to the rest of the class.

Tips for Your Story

- Oral histories are kept alive by being memorable. Keep it simple and stay focused on your story.

- Apply your background knowledge in order to come up with specific and actual instances.

- Be specific. Use concrete details to describe the scene, the actions, and the people.

- If you are the listener, pay attention to the speaker's words and details, as well as his or her voice and gestures.

**Lesson 3
Can anyone
be a hero?**

Vocabulary

Important Words

attributes: the qualities or characteristics of a particular person, place, or thing (*cognate: atributos*)

illustrate: to provide pictures of an idea or to give examples of it (*cognate: ilustrar*)

legendary: being famous because of a special talent or skill (*cognate: legendario*)

selflessness: the act of putting the needs or wishes of other people ahead of your own

Concept Words

concerns: worries or fears

superhero: a fictional heroic character (*cognate: superhéroe*)

superpowers: very strong powers

Superheroes

Dialogue

Two teens are discussing superheroes. Read the dialogue. Then, review the vocabulary words you read.

Teen 1: Who is your favorite superhero?

Teen 2: Mr. Fantastic from the Fantastic Four, for sure. He has the best attributes out of any of the Fantastic Four: stretchy limbs.

Teen 1: Stretchy limbs? That's it? I prefer superheroes with a little more substance. Superman's my favorite superhero. Not only are his superpowers legendary, he is an example of selflessness and strength.

Teen 2: When I watch superhero movies or superhero comic books, I don't have many concerns about what the heroes do for society. I just like to watch them do cool, amazing tricks!

Teen 1: You're missing out! Superman illustrates the goodness in all human beings. He wasn't just a superhero, he was an inspiration to many people who needed to be reminded that goodness can prevail. He was created, remember, at a time when it seemed like Adolph Hitler was going to conquer the world.

Teen 2: I hadn't really thought about that. I didn't realize superheroes could do much more than entertain us. Still, you need to watch the Fantastic Four movie with me. Wait until you see what the Human Torch can do!

- -

Talk About It Discuss the question with a partner or in a group. What are some ways that a superhero reflects the concerns of society? Give one example. Fill in the sentence frame.

The superhero, _________________________________, reflects

the concerns of his or her society by _____________________

____.

Read the article. As you read, think about these questions:
- Where do superheroes really come from?
- How are today's superheroes different from earlier heroes?

OUR HERO!

Have you ever wondered where superheroes come from? Obviously they don't really come from the planet Krypton or atomic accidents, but from the imaginations of their creators. In many cases, the attributes and superpowers of a superhero reflect the social and political concerns of their time.

For example, the legendary character Superman was created in 1938. His purpose was to fight for "truth, justice, and the American way." At that time in history, Adolf Hitler was threatening to conquer the world. Superman's example of selflessness and honor inspired many during a difficult time in history. A few years later, when the United States entered World War II, Captain America was created as a defender of U.S. ideals. Creator Joe Simon said, "We were looking for a villain, and Hitler was the villain."

Following the war, Americans had new concerns. They worried about the dangers of new technologies. Superheroes such as the Hulk, the Fantastic Four, and Spiderman got powers from atomic radiation and out-of-control technology. The Hulk's destructive nature was a reflection of what happens when atomic energy is unleashed. The unique powers of the Fantastic Four, however, showed the potentially helpful side to scientific accidents. These characters were able to illustrate how the public's fear of science and technology could be overcome.

Talk About It Discuss the question with a partner or in a group. Why do you think people need superheroes? Use the sentence frame.

People need superheroes because ________________________

____

____ .

Language and Comprehension

Important Words

compare: to show how things are alike or similar (cognate: *comparar*)

contrast: to show how things are different (cognate: *contrastar*)

worldview: the values and beliefs held by a culture

Worldviews The article you just read talked about how superhero characters can represent worldviews of people. A worldview is the perspective from which people understand the world. A worldview can also consist of a culture's values and beliefs. To understand worldviews, you can compare and contrast details that indicate beliefs, or reasons for those beliefs.

Daniel grew up during the World War II era. He and his friends took turns pretending to be Captain America fighting the German army. As in the cartoon, they always made sure Captain America destroyed the German army. This was a belief most Americans had at the time. By comparison, Daniel's daughter Laura grew up after World War II. Her favorite superhero was Wonder Woman, whose golden lasso was designed to make peace by forcing bad people to tell the truth. After World War II, keeping peace was a belief most Americans had.

Details about Daniel	Details about Captain America	Worldview
Grew up during World War II era.	He fought the German army and always won.	Americans believed that their values would win in the end.

Talk About It Discuss the question with a partner or in a group. How did the character, Captain America, reflect the worldview of Americans during World War II?

Extend Language and Comprehension Review the passage above. Then, complete the chart with details.

Details about Laura	Details about Wonder Woman	Worldview
____________________ ____________________ ____________________	____________________ ____________________ ____________________	____________________ ____________________ ____________________

The worldviews represented by Captain America and Wonder Woman are similar because they both ____________________

____.

However, they are different ____________________

____.

Connect to Writing

Write About a Worldview Think about all you have learned in this lesson. What new words did you use? How did you learn to identify and compare worldviews? Talk with a partner about what you learned.

On a separate sheet of paper, write the answers to the following questions:

- What is a worldview?
- How did you identify worldviews in the text?
- How did you compare and contrast worldviews?

If you need help, use the sentence frames.

A worldview is ______________________________________

____.

I identified worldviews by ___________________________

____.

I compared and contrasted worldviews by _______________

____.

Writing Tips
Don't forget to

1. think about how worldviews reflect culture.

2. use new vocabulary words.

3. edit your writing for spelling.

Extension Activity   Writing

Write a Descriptive Essay On a separate sheet of paper or on a computer, write a descriptive essay about someone who is a hero to you. Write about why this person is important to you. Describe how your hero makes you feel. Portray your hero with expressive language, so the reader can imagine your hero exactly as you see the person in your mind.

Tips for Your Essay

- Use vivid and fresh language to describe your hero.
- Make use of your senses: describe sights, smells, sounds, and textures.
- Use the Writing Process Handbook at the end of this book. This will help you with prewriting, drafting, and revising. If you are writing on a computer, follow the directions for your word-processing program.

Lesson 4
Can anyone be a hero?

Vocabulary

Important Words

conduct: to carry out or manage an activity

courage: the mental strength to face a difficult or dangerous situation *(cognate: coraje)*

determination: the strong desire and drive to reach a goal *(cognate: determinación)*

devise: to make something and to figure out how it will work

inherent: relating to the basic nature of a person or thing *(cognate: inherente)*

Concept Words

bravery: a quality that makes you face danger without showing fear

smokejumper: a special kind of firefighter who fights forest fires

wildfire: an unplanned fire that causes damage to forests and other wild areas

Fighting Wildfires

Dialogue

Two teens are talking about wildfires and smokejumpers. Read the dialogue. Then, review the vocabulary you read.

Teen 1: If you could have any summer job, what would it be?

Teen 2: I would be a smokejumper.

Teen 1: What's that?

Teen 2: It's a person trained to fight wildfires across the United States.

Teen 1: Wow, that sounds like hard work. You would need a lot of courage and determination to do that job.

Teen 2: Danger is inherent to the job. That is why bravery is so important. It also takes a lot of knowledge, strength, and training. Smokejumpers have to know how to use special tools, how to conduct controlled fires, and how to devise strategies for stopping raging wildfires. They also need to know how to jump out of airplanes.

Teen 1: That does sound exciting and heroic, but a bit too dangerous for me. Why don't they just let the fires burn?

Teen 2: Because every year fires ruin billions of dollars worth of homes and forests. I guarantee that if a fire was coming toward your house, you would want a team of smokejumpers nearby.

Talk About It Discuss the questions with a partner or in a group. If you could, would you be a smokejumper? Why or why not? Circle your opinion. Then, complete the sentence frame.

I would /would not be a smokejumper because _____________

____

____.

Read the article. As you read, think about these questions:
- Why do people need to control wildfires?
- Why is smokejumping a dangerous job?

LEAPING INTO THE FIRE

Would you jump out of an airplane over a roaring **wildfire**? That's exactly what **smokejumpers** do every year as part of a national wildfire management team. Their job takes an incredible amount of **courage** and **determination** as they attempt to **devise** strategies to control wildfires.

Most wildfires are an **inherent** part of the natural process and are caused by lightning or dry weather. The fires sweep across the prairies or forests clearing the floor of debris, controlling pests and unwanted plants, and leaving the soil rich in nutrients. However, as more people have settled throughout the United States, wildfires threaten homes and waste valuable resources.

In response, the government has developed a national fire plan, which includes the work of smokejumpers and other professionals. Smokejumpers contain wildfires by clearing debris around the fire's edges, or by setting backfires that keep fires from

Smokejumpers are the first line of defense against wildfires.

spreading. Federal agencies also **conduct** controlled burns in certain areas, in the hopes of clearing fuel for potential wildfires. Despite the **bravery** of smokejumpers, wildfires continue to be a problem. In 2007, people in California lost more than $1 billion worth of property. Increased dry weather and hot winds guarantee that smokejumpers will have plenty of work in the future.

Talk About It Discuss the question with a partner or in a group. Is the government doing enough to stop wildfires? Circle your opinion. Then, complete the sentence frame.

I think the federal government is /is not doing enough to stop

wildfires because ____

____.

Important Words

compare: to show how things are alike or similar *(cognate: comparar)*

contrast: to show how things are different *(cognate: contrastar)*

worldview: the values and beliefs held by a culture

Different Worldviews A worldview is the perspective with which a character, the author, or a group of people understand the world. To understand worldviews, look for details that indicate values and beliefs, or reasons for those beliefs. Sometimes, a piece of writing will reflect several worldviews. You can understand worldviews when you compare and contrast them.

Talk About It Discuss the questions with a partner or in a group. What do you do when you compare things? What do you do when you contrast things?

Extend Language and Comprehension A Venn diagram can help you compare and contrast worldviews. Read the passage. Then, compare the worldviews of the two characters.

As a former smokejumper, Bob has seen the devastation caused by wildfires. He survived fires that took the lives of fellow smokejumpers, burned millions of acres of timber, and destroyed hundreds of homes. He says proudly, "Smokejumping isn't just necessary, it creates a courage that takes you through life." While his son Chad admires his father's bravery and persistence, his career has taken him in different directions. He sees that wildfires are a necessary part of nature, and that most of his father's work was designed to save human settlements. Chad works to stop human changes to the environment that cause wildfires.

- How are the worldviews of Bob and Chad alike?
- How are the worldviews of Bob and Chad different?

Bob's worldview **Chad's worldview**

Differences   Similarities   Differences

Connect to Writing

Write About Different Worldviews Think about all you have learned in this lesson. What new words did you use? How did you learn to identify and compare and contrast worldviews? Talk with a partner about what you learned.

On a separate sheet of paper, compare and contrast worldviews you encountered in this lesson. Write the answers to the following questions:

- What worldviews did you find which related to the topic of the article, "Leaping into the Fire"?
- How were the worldviews similar?
- How were the worldviews different?

If you need help, use the sentence frames.

> One worldview I found was ________________________________
>
> ____.
>
> This compared to another worldview ______________________
>
> ____.
>
> They were similar in that the worldviews both _____________
>
> ____.
>
> However, they differed _________________________________
>
> ____.

Writing Tips

Don't forget to

1. think about details that reveal worldviews.

2. use compare and contrast words.

3. edit for correct punctuation.

Connect to the Big Question 

Think about all the articles you read in this unit. Which article did you like best? Which article did you not like? Then, think about your favorite article and say what the article was about.

Now, take some time to share your final ideas. Answer this question: How can regular people be heroes? Complete the sentence frame below.

> Regular people can be heroes by _______________________
>
> ____
>
> ____.

Can anyone be a hero?

Big Question Words and Important Words

attributes

character

conceive

conduct

consult

courage

determination

devise

illustrate

inherent

integrity

irony

legendary

persevere

responsibility

sacrifice

selflessness

Vocabulary Review

Best Definition Read the sentence. Circle the best definition for each underlined word.

1. The scientist could not <u>conceive</u> of unleashing atomic energy on the world.
   A. consult
   B. devise
   C. think
   D. persevere

2. She had the <u>courage</u> to jump from an airplane into a fire.
   A. mental strength
   B. strong desire
   C. responsibility
   D. sacrifice

3. Of all the superheroes, Superman is the most <u>legendary</u>.
   A. ironic
   B. famous
   C. selfless
   D. responsible

4. Often, superheroes <u>illustrate</u> how to be courageous.
   A. give advice about
   B. give meaning to
   C. show sacrifices of
   D. give examples of

5. I was impressed by the robot's human <u>attributes</u>.
   A. selflessness
   B. determination
   C. characteristics
   D. confrontation

Personal Response Complete each sentence with your response.

1. I want to be legendary for _______________________________

   ____.

2. The best sacrifice I ever made was _______________________

   ____.

3. I have a lot of determination for ________________________

   ____.

4. It is a big responsibility to ____________________________

   ____.

5. I want to conduct an experiment about ___________________

   ____.

Comprehension Review

Cultural and Historical Context Cultural and historical context refers to the specific events, beliefs, and customs that reflect the time and culture of a story or article. Read the passage below. Then, fill in the chart.

After telling his story to the class, the old Lakota man sat back and smiled. Tears streamed down his face. "It is important to pass on oral traditions," he said. "A long time ago, people tried to remove our traditions, but we did not let that happen. That is why I thank you for listening to what I said today."

Cultural and Historical Context	Examples from the text
time and place	
events	
beliefs and customs	
language	

Compare and Contrast Worldviews A worldview is the perspective from which a character, an author, or a group of people understand the world. Fill in the chart below. Compare and contrast the worldviews reflected by Batman and Captain America.

In 1939, the character Batman was created. Although he didn't have superpowers, he used his intelligence and advanced technology to defeat enemies. Captain America soon followed in 1941, except that his character was created specifically to depict an American hero fighting enemy armies in World War II. He used both superhuman strength, provided by a "super soldier" formula, and special weapons like a bulletproof shield to defeat enemies.

Superhero	Details from text	Worldview
Batman		
Captain America		

Can anyone be a hero?

In this unit, I read:

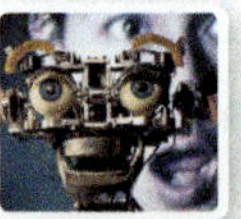

In this unit, I:

- learned new vocabulary words.
- read about different topics.
- identified cultural context.
- used my background knowledge.
- learned about worldviews.
- learned about cultural context.
- compared and contrasted worldviews.
- wrote about cultural context.
- conducted a debate.
- wrote about background knowledge.
- told a story.
- wrote about worldviews.
- wrote a descriptive essay.

Reflection Think about what you learned in this unit. Complete each sentence frame. Share your answers with your teacher and classmates.

I wonder ____.

I learned ____.

I discovered ____.

I still want to know ____.

I still don't understand ____.

Table of Contents

The Writing Process

You write every day. You may have e-mailed a friend. You may have made a list of all the things you need to do today. You may have worked on a school assignment. They are all forms of writing. Now it is time to move on to a bigger writing project.

Use the information about the writing process in this handbook to write an essay or a story. The writing process takes you step by step from choosing a topic, to publishing, or presenting, what you have written.

The Writing Process

Use these five steps to write your essay.

1 Prewriting Brainstorm topic ideas, choose a topic, do research, and organize details before you begin writing.

2 Drafting Write your ideas down on paper roughly in the way you planned.

3 Revising Read your first draft and look to find ways you can make it better or more interesting. Then, revise it. Revise means to make changes.

4 Editing and Proofreading Correct errors in grammar, spelling, and mechanics.

5 Publishing and Presenting Share your writing with others.

Talk About It Discuss these questions with a partner or a small group of classmates. Which step in the writing process do you like the best? Which step do you think is the most challenging? Complete the sentence frames.

The step in the writing process I like best is ________________________

because ____

____.

The most challenging step for me is ________________________________

____

because ____

____.

1 Prewriting

Prewriting is all the things you do before you begin to write. Follow the prewriting activities in the chart below. Use a separate sheet of paper for your writing. You can read the information below with a partner.

Getting Ready to Write

Choose a topic
Write down all the topic ideas you think of or brainstorm for ideas with classmates. You can also choose one of the topics from the list. Look over all your topic ideas. You may choose the one you know the most about.

Remember your audience
Your audience is the person or people who will read what you write. Is it your teacher? a friend? the principal? Knowing your audience usually changes the way you write and the words you use.

Choose a purpose
There are four main purposes for reading. They are to inform, to persuade, to entertain, and to reflect. Choose the purpose that best fits your topic.

Gather resources and information
When you gather details, you collect information on your topic. As you do this, make sure your topic is not too big or too small. Don't limit detail gathering to your own experiences and knowledge. You may need to do library research, search the Internet, or interview others to collect the information you need. Take notes on the information you will need in order to start writing.

Topic Ideas

endangered animals

recycling

Olympic games

hip hop

natural disasters

Organize Ideas

Use the information you learned to complete this prewriting chart.

I'm Ready to Write
Topic:
Audience:
Purpose:
Resources and Information:

2 Drafting

A draft is where you get all your ideas down on paper. The prewriting activities have prepared you for this, so you should do well. Take a quick look back at your topic and the details you have gathered. Focus on your main ideas, interesting details, plot and setting (if you are writing a story), and your audience. You can organize your information in an outline to help you write your draft.

Now, take out a sheet of paper, pick up a pencil, and start writing. The goal of a first draft is to write your paper from beginning to end. Don't worry about mistakes. You'll have plenty of time to fix them later. Remember, even the best writers don't expect their first draft to be perfect. The important thing about writing a draft is that it gives you something to work on—and make better.

Details, Details, Details

Make your writing clear by supporting your main ideas with enough details. Details help readers understand your ideas. If you need help adding details, you may want to use the **SEE** method.

In the **SEE** method, you start with a statement of your main idea. Then, you extend it with more details that relate to the main idea. Finally, you elaborate or apply more details to the main idea. Look at the example below. The topic of this essay is how baby elephants grow to be adults.

STATEMENT Baby elephants have a lot to learn.

EXTENSION The baby elephant has to be taught how to use its trunk—much like a human baby has to learn how to walk or use a spoon.

ELABORATION It takes baby elephants many years to learn how to communicate, and how to survive.

Talk About It Discuss these questions with a partner or a small group of classmates. What topics would you find very interesting to write about? What kind of details would you like to include in your writing that weren't there before? Complete the sentence frames.

Writing a draft was helpful because ________________________________

____.

I would want to add details such as ________________________________

____.

3 Revising

You make changes when you revise. You reread your draft to find places where you need to fix what you wrote. You ask yourself questions such as the ones on the list.

As you review your writing, mark the places you need to revise. Some revisions you can write directly on your draft. If it is a word or sentence you want to change, just put a line through it. Then, write the new word or sentence above it. You can also make notes to yourself in the margins or on another sheet of paper.

When you are done, write a corrected, or revised, version of your first draft essay or story.

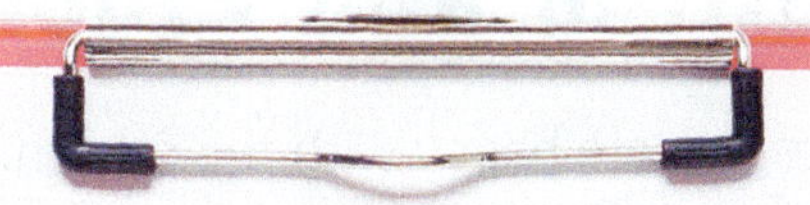

Buddy Review

As part of your revision, you can ask one or two people to read your writing. Ask them to tell you what they liked best about your draft, and what they liked least. Have the readers show you the places they may have been confused. You might even ask them if they have any suggestions for improvement. Thank them for their ideas. Then, decide what revisions you will make.

Writing Tips

Many word processing programs have built-in thesauruses to help writers improve their drafts. Highlight a word and use the thesaurus to preview a list of other words with similar meanings. Use a variety of words instead of repeating the same ones. This can make your writing more interesting.

4 Editing and Proofreading

Once you are happy with the content of your writing, it is time to edit and proofread. This means you carefully read your writing and look for mistakes in grammar, punctuation, usage, and mechanics. Here are some things you should look for as you proofread.

Proofreading Checklist

Spelling
Use a dictionary to check the spelling of any word that you are not sure is spelled correctly.

Capitalization and Punctuation
Make sure every sentence begins with a capital letter and has a period, question mark, or exclamation point at the end. Then, look at other punctuation you have used.

Grammar and Usage Conventions
Be sure you have corrected sentence fragments and that the subject and verb of every sentence agrees.

Fact Check
Be sure the facts and ideas you include in your writing are true. Use the accuracy checklist shown on this page.

Handwriting
Make sure your handwriting is readable. Rewrite any words that may be difficult for another reader to understand.

Accuracy Checklist

✓ Names

✓ Dates and titles

✓ Statistics

✓ Exact wording of quotations

✓ Ideas that are not your own

Talk About It Discuss the Accuracy Checklist with a partner or a small group of classmates. In your own writing, how would you check to see if the items listed were true? Complete the sentence frame.

I would check to see if they were true by __________________________

____

____.

5 Publishing and Presenting

Now it's time to share your writing with others.

Finalize Your Writing

You may want to type your work on a computer. This will let you make copies to share. When you use a word-processing program, choose a font that is easy to read. You might want to add pictures, drawings, diagrams, charts, or graphs to your writing. These visuals may help your readers understand your topic.

Make Your Own Portfolio

You have done a lot of hard work and it shows what you can do. Put your work in a portfolio—a folder, box, file, or a safe container. Save place in your portfolio for writing ideas, photos, and other things that inspire you.

Make a Bibliography

For some kinds of writing, you need to list citations that tell readers where you found your information. If you write a research paper, you make a bibliography to tell readers what sources you used. A bibliography follows a specific format. It tells readers the name of the title, author, and publisher of a source. It also shows what date the information was published.

> **Book:** Author's Last Name, Author's First Name. Book Title. Publisher's City: Publisher's Name, Year.
>
> London, Jack. *The Call of the Wild*. New York: Scholastic, 2001.
>
> **Magazine:** Author's Last Name, Author's First Name. "Article Title." Magazine Title. Volume Date: Page numbers.
>
> Young, Diane. "At the High End of the River." *Southern Living*. June 2000: 126-131.
>
> **Website:** Article Title. Date accessed. URL
>
> Circle of Stories. 25 Jan. 2006. http://www.pbs.org/circleofstories/

Writing Tips

Here are just a few suggestions for how you can share your writing. In addition to reading it to your class, you can send it to a newspaper or magazine. You can read it to your family and neighbors. You could also put it on a bulletin board in your classroom or in the school for all to see.

Word List

affect
effect

imminent
eminent

persecuted
prosecuted

apprise
appraise

illicit
elicit

Easily Confused Words

Certain words are easily confused with each other. They may sound similar, have related meanings or have similar spellings.

Choosing the Correct Word The Word List contains five pairs of words. The two words in each pair are easy to confuse and can often cause spelling errors in your work. If you use one in place of the other, a spell-checker won't pick up on these errors. Don't rely only on spell-checkers programs, but proofread your work closely.

Use a dictionary to determine the difference between the words in each pair. Then, study the Word List until you are sure you understand the difference between the two words.

Practice Read each of the following sentences. Then, fill in the letters necessary to complete the correct word from the word pairs.

1. The criminal was _____ _____ _____secuted for his crime.

2. The weather will _____ffect our plans for the picnic.

3. The _____ffect of the Internet is improved communication.

4. The flashing light indicated a power failure was _____ _____ _____inent.

5. We tried to _____ _____icit a smile from the baby.

6. We have art experts app_____ _____ _____ _____ the painting.

7. When a group is _____ _____ _____secuted, its members may fear for their lives.

8. _____ _____ _____icit activities are usually criminal activities.

9. He is an _____ _____inent statesman and won the Nobel Peace Prize last year.

10. Did they appr_____ _____e you of the time that the meeting starts?

Assessment Practice

Directions Write the letter of the sentence in which all the words are spelled correctly.

1. A. The affact of the new road was to speed up traffic
   B. Did my argument affecte your decision?
   C. The bright green wall had a strange effect on the light in the room.
   D. the effecte of the treaty isn't known.

2. A. The district attorney persecuted the case.
   B. Certain crimes against the community will always be persacuted.
   C. He felt persecuted when they would not stop laughing at him.
   D. The protesters were persequeted for obstructing traffic on the highway.

3. A. Please appraize the value of this antique.
   B. Will someone apprase David of the homework assignment.
   C. Marla can apraise you of what happened at the meeting.
   D. Who can appraise the book's value?

4. A. A good moderator can elicit a response from anybody.
   B. There is a large elicet market in stolen bicycles.
   C. The executive stored his ellicit gains in a foreign bank account.
   D. We tried to elisit information from the children.

· ·

Directions Write the letter of the correct spelling of the word that best completes the sentence.

1. The time to make up your mind is __________.
   A. iminent   C. imminent
   B. eminent   D. emminent

2. It will be hard to __________ the case without witnesses.
   A. persecute   C. prosacute
   B. prosecute   D. presecute

3. The antibiotic had no __________ on her illness.
   A. afect   C. affect
   B. efect   D. effect

4. Penguins do not live in the __________ region.
   A. artic   C. arctick
   B. arctic   D. artick

5. The boat smuggled the __________ cargo past the guards.
   A. ilicit   C. illicit
   B. elicit   D. illisit

6. The __________ judge was respected by everyone.
   A. iminent   C. imminent
   B. eminent   D. emminent

Word List

- villain
- liaison
- guarantee
- cantaloupe
- counterfeit
- porcelain
- vacuum
- waive
- lieutenant
- camouflage

Vowel Combinations

Certain words are difficult to spell because they have unusual letter combinations. Some of these combinations involve vowels.

Did You Use the Right Vowel? Some of the vowel sounds in the words on the Word List are silent. Silent vowels in combination of vowels that you hear can make spelling correctly difficult. In most cases, two vowels are used to spell a sound that usually takes only one vowel. For example, look at the words porcel**ai**n and counterf**ei**t.

Read through the Word List and look at the vowel groupings. If a word gives you problems, make up a mnemonic device, or memory aid, to help you remember to include all the letters. A mnemonic device can be a sentence, a rhyme, or another trick to help you.

Example: A *u* hides in *camouflage*.

Practice Match the vowel combinations to correctly spell the words on the Word List.

1. ieuea _______________________________

2. aaoue _______________________________

3. iai _______________________________

4. aie _______________________________

5. aouae _______________________________

6. auu _______________________________

7. iaio _______________________________

8. uaaee _______________________________

9. oeai _______________________________

10. oueei _______________________________

Assessment Practice

Directions Write the letter of the sentence in which the underlined word is spelled correctly.

1. A. A He was the <u>villin</u> of the story.
   B. He had been a <u>luetenent</u>.
   C. He got into trouble trying to pass <u>counterfeit</u> money.
   D. He was caught when he could not <u>garantee</u> that it was genuine.

2. A. A The <u>porceline</u> bowl fell the to the floor.
   B. In it were several slices of <u>cantaloupe</u>.
   C. We tried to <u>camoflage</u> the damage.
   D. We cleaned up with a <u>vacume</u>.

3. A. A Derek is the school's <u>laiason</u> with the city.
   B. He asked the council to <u>wave</u> the late fee.
   C. They refused to <u>guarantey</u> cooperation.
   D. They feared the students would <u>camouflage</u> their recent earnings.

4. A. A The museum received a <u>vaccuum</u>-packed article.
   B. They were told that it was a <u>porcelain</u> vase.
   C. The vase was a <u>counterfit</u>.
   D. They never found out what <u>villian</u> had tried to trick them.

· ·

Directions Write in the letter of the correct spelling of the word.

1. Marta finds _______________ work interesting.
   A. laiason   C. liaison
   B. laiaison   D. liaeson

2. They will _______________ all fees for kids under 12.
   A. waive   C. waeve
   B. wave   D. whaive

3. Judy wants to be a _______________ commander.
   A. lootenent   C. lieutenant
   B. lieutenent   D. leiutenant

4. Please eat some of that _______________
   A. cantalaupe   C. cantaoope
   B. cantaloupe   D. cantaluope

5. They can _______________ the wall with tree branches.
   A. camoflage   C. camoeflage
   B. caumoflage   D. camouflage

6. Dave will _______________ the living room.
   A. vacuum   C. vaccuum
   B. vaccume   D. vacumme

Tools For Checking Spelling

Word List

- capital
- capitol
- emphasize
- graphic
- hypothesize
- analyze
- knowledge
- composition
- yield
- miscellaneous

Computer Spell-Checkers Always run spell check on electronic documents when you are finished writing them. However, remember that no spell-checker will catch all mistakes. Watch out for the following errors:

- Programs cannot tell you if you used the wrong homophone— a word with the same pronunciation as the word you meant, but with a different spelling.

- Programs cannot tell you if you have typed another, unrelated word. For example, you might type gone when you meant to type done.

Dictionaries When looking up a word in the dictionary, keep in mind that some sounds can be spelled in more than one way. For example, in *age*, *just*, and *trudge*, the *j* sound is spelled three different ways.

Practice Use a dictionary to find the correct spelling of each word. Write the word correctly.

1. misselaneous

____

2. yeild

____

3. philosofy

____

4. compasision

____

5. emphasise

____

6. competision

____

7. hipothisise

____

8. graffic

____

9. analize

____

Rewrite each sentence, spelling all words correctly. Use a dictionary to check the meaning of homophones. Tell whether a spell-checker program would catch the errors, and explain why or why not.

1. We visited the state capital building. _______________

____

2. The zoo had and antelope and a zebra. _______________

____

3. Use a capitol letter to start a sentence. _______________

____

Assessment Practice

Directions On your paper, write the number of the sentence and all the spelling corrections it needs. If a sentence has no errors, write "None." Use a dictionary for help.

1. The movie that we watched was set in the fuedal era.

2. Until I saw that film, I could not conceive how different life was several hundred years ago.

3. There is a great khasm between that period—the age of shivalry—and now.

4. In the movie, most of the people lived is a tiny village.

5. This pictureskque location was part of the estate of a wealthy lord.

6. This ruler had control over the land, and people worked for him.

7. When times were good, their storehouses teamed with grain.

8. When there was a bleight, people starved.

9. Health and higene were chronic problems.

10. Across the years, the routine of life changed very little.

11. On pleasant evenings, people sat around the fire and tolled stories.

12. Sometimes, they made up rhymes about great heroes from the past.

13. The landowner also lived quietly.

14. He ate what the peasants grew in the fields, but he received his food on peuter platters.

. . . .

Directions Rewrite each sentence, spelling all words correctly. Use a dictionary for help.

1. We used a grafic to analize the information.

2. He wrote a composition about the capitol city.

3. You can use capitol letters to emphasize a word.

4. Scientists combine knowlege and experiments to hypothosyze.

5. The research will yeild missellaneous facts.

Word List

characterize

compromise

advertise

merchandise

memorize

analyze

publicize

realize

hypothesize

symbolize

Words With Similar Endings: *-ize, -ise, -yze*

Endings that sound the same or almost the same can be tricky to spell. How do you choose among the endings *-ize, -ise,* and *-yze*?

Spell the Ending Correctly The endings *-ize, -ise,* and *-yze* can all be pronounced "iz."

- Usually, *-ize* is a suffix added to another word to make a verb, as is the case with

  civilize   and   **characterize**.
  civil + ***-ize***   **character** + ***ize***

For words with one of the other two endings, there are no set rules, so you will have to memorize which words use which spellings. Make a list in your notebook of the words that give you trouble, and refer to it or a dictionary if you are unsure of the spelling of a word.

Practice On a separate piece of paper, write the word from the Word List that is related to each word below. Underline any changes where a spelling change happens when the suffixes is added. Explain the change.

1. vtaeiesdry _______________________________

2. zaaienyl _______________________________

3. leerzisa _______________________________

4. heriacrzeacty _______________________________

5. ezsimorpmoc _______________________________

6. zsipotheheys _______________________________

7. diyseerchman _______________________________

8. scuzeblipy _______________________________

9. immezoers _______________________________

10. zaboyimles _______________________________

Assessment Practice

Directions For each item, write the letters of the words that are incorrectly spelled. If all the underlined words are correct, choose (D) No error.

1. We are working hard to <u>publicize</u> the <u>store's</u> <u>merchandize</u>. <u>No error</u>.
                                    A.   B.   C.   D.

2. The <u>students</u> <u>realize</u> that they must <u>memorise</u> the rules. <u>No error</u>.
       A.   B.   C.   D.

3. The committee members <u>finally</u> <u>anayzed</u> the problem and reached a
                                A.   B.
<u>compromise</u>. <u>No error</u>.
   C.   D.

4. We <u>hypothesised</u> that the author <u>symbolized</u> the trial so the work would
        A.   B.
get <u>passed</u> the censors. <u>No error</u>.
     C.   D.

· ·

Directions Write the letter of the word that has the correct spelling to fill in the blank.

1. Was it difficult to ________________ the chemical equations?
   - A. memorise
   - B. memoryze
   - C. memoreyes
   - D. memorize

2. I did not ________________ that we were leaving so early.
   - A. reelize
   - B. reelise
   - C. realize
   - D. realise

3. We will never get a contract unless you ________________
   - A. compromise
   - B. compramise
   - C. compromize
   - D. compromice

4. The skills needed to ________________ literature are higher-level thinking skills.
   - A. analize
   - B. ananlyze
   - C. analyze
   - D. analyse

5. How would you ________________ our new neighbor?
   - A. caracterize
   - B. characterise
   - C. characterice
   - D. characterize

6. The ________________ behind his argument is weak.
   - A. premese
   - B. premise
   - C. premice
   - D. premize

Word List

- commitment
- embarrass
- accommodations
- questionnaire
- appalling
- connoisseur
- harass
- millennium
- bookkeeper
- dilemma

Words with Double Letters

Words with one or more sets of double letters are common in English. Some of these words can cause spelling problems even for good spellers.

Seeing Double Words with double letters can cause all sorts of spelling problems. If a word has one set of double letters, like **dilemma**, it is often hard to remember which letter to double. If a word has two or more sets of double letters, like **embarrass**, people tend to forget to double one of them. Look carefully at the words on the list, and make up clues to help you remember any that you tend to spell wrong.

Practice Read the clues that tell how many times the given letters appear in each word. Write the word from the Word List that matches the clue. Use each word only once.

1. l-2, n-2 __________________________

2. p-2, l-2 __________________________

3. r-2, s-2 __________________________

4. k-2, p-1 __________________________

5. r-1, s-2 __________________________

6. c-2, m-2 __________________________

7. l-1, m-2 __________________________

8. m-2, t-1, m-1, t-1 __________________________

9. t-1, n-2, r-1 __________________________

10. n-2, s-2 __________________________

Assessment Practice

Directions Write the letter of the sentence in which the underlined word is spelled correctly.

1. A. A each member received a
      <u>questionairre</u>.
   B. Did the officers mean to <u>embarass</u> us
      with some of the things they asked?
   C. For example, they asked us about our
      <u>committment</u> to education.
   D. Wouldn't it be <u>appalling</u> if no one
      answered?

2. A. A few years ago, office workers
      faced a <u>dillema</u>.
   B. Not only a new century, but a new
      <u>milennium</u> began.
   C. Every <u>bookkeeper</u> needed to change
      dates from 19_ _ to 20_ _.
   D. Was it fair to <u>harrass</u> employees who
      forgot to fix their own records?

3. A. The <u>conoisseur</u> liked to travel
      in style.
   B. The <u>accomodations</u> he chose were
      always the finest.
   C. He also had a <u>commitment</u> to dining
      at the best restaurants.
   D. Clearly, spending huge amounts of
      money did not <u>embarras</u> him.

4. A. A Tour guides must sometimes deal
      with a <u>dillemma</u>.
   B. They know that unruly travelers
      sometimes <u>harass</u> others on the trips.
   C. Should they request separate
      <u>acomodations</u> for these tourists?
   D. After all, it would be <u>apalling</u> if
      another tourist's trip were ruined by
      one lout's rudeness.

- -

Directions Write the letter of the correct spelling that completes the sentence.

1. Only a few generations are able to
   witness a new _______________.
   A. millennium   C. millenium
   B. millennium   D. milenium

2. She is a _______________ of
   classical music.
   A. connoisseur   C. connoiseur
   B. conoiseur   D. conoisseur

3. A long _______________ came in
   the mail.
   A. questionair   C. questionnaire
   B. questionnair   D. questionaire

4. It was a _______________ because both
   events were on the same day.
   A. dillemma   C. dillema
   B. dilema   D. dilemma

5. I am _______________ by their rude
   behavior.
   A. embarassed   C. embarassed
   B. embarrazed   D. embarrassed

6. We can't find _______________;
   all the lodging is booked.
   A. acomodations   C. accommodations
   B. acommodations   D. accomodations

Word List

- emigrate
- immigrate
- transmittal
- reevaluate
- liveliness
- irreplaceable
- machinations
- specious
- concede
- dissemble

Spelling on College Entrance Exams

You will find a few spelling items in the English section of most college entrance exams. To do well on them, look for small, easy errors; recall some basic rules; and know your own spelling problems.

Testing Tip Though spelling is not the most important part of college entrance exams, spelling items do occur in writing or English usage sections of most tests. The following recommendations will help you prepare for items of this type.

- Look for homophone errors, easily confused words, or simple words spelled incorrectly. Remember, for example, that **who's**, not **whose** is the correct spelling for the contraction **"who is."**

- Review word formation rules that people sometimes forget.

- When adding endings to multi-syllable words whose final letters are a vowel followed by a consonant, double the final consonant if the accent is on the final syllable.

- When adding prefixes to words, do not drop any letters.

- When adding suffixes to words ending in **consonant** + **y**, remember that the final **y** usually changes to **i**.

- In words ending in **consonant** + **e**, the final **e** is usually dropped when the suffix begins with a vowel—but not when the base word ends in **ce** or **ge**.

- Know the words that give you trouble and work out memory tricks to help with them. If you cannot remember where the **y** comes in **rhythm**, try making a saying with the letters **r-h-y**, or just remember the letter group.

Assessment Practice

Directions Write the letter of the item that contains a spelling, punctuation, capitalization, or usage error. Write "(E) No error" if there are no errors in the sentence.

1. Although I knew that <u>Professor Chin</u> was <u>infuriated</u>, she <u>manages</u> to
                  A.   B.   C.
   <u>dissemble</u> her true feelings with a smile. <u>No error.</u>
   D.   E.

2. The <u>women's</u> choir sang traditional <u>American</u> songs with a <u>livliness</u> that
      A.   B.   C.
   had the audience clapping <u>their</u> hands and singing along. <u>No error.</u>
                   D.   E.

3. The judge though that <u>Lewis Davis, Jr.</u>, a known <u>criminal</u>, would offer a
                   A.   B.
   <u>specious</u> story about his <u>whereabouts; however,</u> he said nothing.
    C.   D.
   <u>No error.</u>
    E.

4. Voters were fed up with the <u>mackinations</u> of the ruling <u>party</u>, an arrogant
                      A.   B.
   group <u>whose</u> members were only interested in staying in office and <u>filling</u>
        C.   D.
   their own pockets. <u>No error.</u>
                  E.

Directions Write the letter of the version of the underlined section that makes the item correct and appropriate. If you think the original version is best, choose "No Change."

1. Boris knew that the papers of <u>transmittal were irreplaceable,</u> since they allowed <u>his family to immigrate.</u> 2. However, he could not find them anywhere. 3. After much frantic <u>searching, he had to conceed</u> that they were lost. 4. With a heavy heart, <u>he begins to reevaluate</u> his plans for leaving Lutonia.

1. A. No Change
   B. transmittal was irreplaceable, since
   C. transmital were irreplaceable, since
   D. transmittal were irreplaceable, though

2. A. No Change
   B. their family to immigrate
   C. his family to emigrate
   D. their family to emigrate

3. A. No Change
   B. searching he had to conceed
   C. searching, they had to conceed
   D. searching, he had to concede

4. A. No Change
   B. he began to reevaluate
   C. he begins to revaluate
   D. he began to revaluate

An Introduction to Informational Text

This year you will be reading different types of informational text in your Reading and Language Arts class. These pages contain definitions and examples of the different kinds of information you will read with your teacher and classmates. If you have questions during the school year or need help understanding the purpose of various informational texts, you can refer back to these pages.

Different Types of Informational Materials

Here are some definitions for different kinds of informational materials:

advertisement a notice designed to attract your attention and usually meant to sell a product

news article a piece of writing on a certain topic that appears in a newspaper or magazine

rental agreement or contract an official document that lets you rent or borrow something like an apartment or car, in exchange for money

warranty/insurance policy a contract that allows people to receive compensation for defects or damage to something they own

employment application a written request for a job. A listing of your personal information and work experience

business letter a formal exchange between two people about their professional interests

Instruction manual contains step-by-step directions for finishing a task

Talk About It Discuss the the different types of informational materials with a partner or in a small group. Are you familiar with any of these examples? How did you learn about them? Now, complete the sentence frame.

I have read ____

because I was interested in ______________________________________

____.

It was useful to me because ______________________________________

____.

Advertisement

An **advertisement** in print or on the web usually gives you information about a product or service. It may show a picture of the product you can buy. Often, information is provided, such as an item description and the cost. Sometimes there is a company name, address, telephone number, and web site listed.

Talk About It With a partner or in a small group, search through newspapers and magazines for interesting advertisements. Why are they appealing? What visual elements catch your attention? What words are used to encourage you to buy the product? How does the repetition of words or phrases help convince you? Complete the sentence frame and present your ideas to the class.

I was interested in buying ____

when I saw an ad for it. I liked this ad because the information was

____.

The repetition of the words ____________________________________

would convince me to buy this because ___________________________

____.

News Article

News articles give readers information about a particular subject or area of interest, such as current events, travel, sports, or entertainment.

The **byline** shows the name of the person who wrote the article.

The **headline** tells you the subject of the article.

Articles may include **quotations** from people involved in the news.

Bike Trip Around the World

Derek Cowner
Greytown Times Staff Writer

GREYTOWN Many people dream of "leaving it all behind." One couple has decided to do just that. Anthony and Lydia Giles, at the ages of 55 and 45, have sold their business, their home, their cars, and donated almost all of their possessions. Almost, except for what they could strap on the back of their bicycles. They are headed for a bicycle adventure around the world.

"We have no idea what to expect, but we know it will be life-changing," Anthony Giles says. "We're anxious and excited to see what's out there."

The couple has been considering an extended bike trip for years, but it wasn't until one of them had a health-scare that they finally resolved to do it. In 2007, Lydia suffered a heart attack. "The day after the heart attack I thought, 'This is it---this is the time to go.' I realized that we don't have forever."

Their plans are rough. Instead of a carefully laid-out plan with fixed dates, the couple has only a starting point and a stack of guidebooks and maps. "We want this trip to be open," Anthony says. "We'll make our trip as we go along. It's more exciting that way."

While Anthony and Lydia characterize their trip as "adventurous," their friends characterize it as something else. Carol, a former employee of the couple's business, who will be throwing a party for the couple the day before they leave, says, "Most of us think they're crazy! But we're all looking forward to the pictures."

Talk About It Find examples of news articles and read them with a partner. Discuss the articles and the features of a news article. What kinds of news stories interest you the most? Why? Complete the sentence frame with your answers.

I have read news articles about _______________________________________

____

because I was interested in ____.

I learned the following key ideas, details, and facts: _________________

____

Rental Agreement

A **rental agreement** is a document that lists the responsibilities and duties you must follow in order to rent or borrow something. It may be a **contract** for an apartment, a car, or some other product. Rental agreements are based on laws and involve an exchange of money for the product or service.

BICYCLE CITY
BICYCLE RENTAL FORM

DATE OF USE: ______________	☐ Full Day ☐ ½ Day ☐ Other ________
Name (Renter):	Group Name:

***Renter shall be held liable for damages or loss of any rental equipment

Street Address:

City, State, Zip:

Home Phone Number:	Cell Phone Number:

	Equipment	Quantity	Unit Rate	Total Cost
☐	Bicycle		$15/half day - $25 full day	
☐	Helmet		$5/half day - $10 full day	
☐	Lock		$3/half day - $15 full day	
☐	Child Carriers		$10/half day - $15 full day	

Total Paid:	☐ Cash ☐ Check # __________

Price The agreement lists the money owed for the rental.

BICYCLE CITY - Bicycle Rental Forms

Bicycle Safety Tips and Release of Responsibility
- **All bicycle riders must wear a helmet.**
- **Young children must wear helmets and be seated in child carriers.**
- **An adult must sign rental forms for bicyclists under 18.**
- **Bicycle riders must obey all traffic laws.**
- **Extra charges will added if bicycles are not returned on time.**

Release of Responsibility: Bicycle City does not take responsibilibty for any injuries, accidents or lost articles. Renter assumes responsibility for all risks.

I have read and understood the above Bicycle Safety Tips and Release of Responsibility and agree to follow them. Additionally, I agree to pay all costs for damaged equipment rented by me.

Renter's Name: _______________________ **Date:** ____________

Agreement terms say what is being rented and what the expectations are.

Talk About It Discuss these questions with a partner or in a small group of classmates. If you were to rent something, what would it be? Why? Then, discuss why agreements are important. Complete the sentence frame with your answers.

I would be interested in renting a(n) ____________________________

because ____.

Agreements are important because ____________________________

____.

Warranty/Insurance Policy

A **warranty** is a written guarantee that your purchase is in good condition and will be replaced or repaired if it is found defective. An **insurance policy** is a formal contract that protects a person or a piece of property and guarantees that a person will receive payment for any damages.

This coverage notice shows what expenses will be paid for if damage occur to the bicycle or bicycle parts.

PART OF A BICYCLE WARRANTY FROM BIKERIDE, INC.

Part A—Liability Coverage

A Warranty coverage on the frame of the bicycle covers the life of the bicycle as long as it is owned by the original purchaser. BikeRide warranty coverage on the bicycle components (excluding tubes, tires, and cables;) covers one year as long as the bicycle is owned by the original retail purchaser.

BikeRide's five-year warranty coverage includes:
Aluminum frames
Products made prior to January 2007

BikeRide's one-year coverage includes the following models and frames:
Downhill models
Jumping models
Freestyle models
Suspension related equipment (bolts, pivot pins, bushings, bearings.)

Exclusions are things not covered by this bike insurance policy.

Exclusions
BikeRide warranty does not cover the following:

1. Damage, or loss of bike caused by stunt riding, ramp jumping, or other similar activities.
2. Bending of frames, handlebars, seat posts, or wheel rims. (These can be a sign of abuse or misuse of bicycle.)
3. Labor charges connected with the repair or replacement of all parts. Shipment or transportation to or from an authorized BikeRide dealer.

Labor charges means charges made for time bike mechanic spends on carrying out repairs.

Talk About It Discuss the question with a partner or in a small group. What kinds of things would need a warranty or an insurance policy? Complete the sentence frame with your answers. Discuss key words used that identify the purpose of the warranty or policy.

It is important to have a warranty for products like _________________

____

because ____.

Insurance policies are useful for products like cars and houses because ____

____.

IC5

Employment Application

An **employment application** is a written request for a job that requires a person to provide personal background information, related work experience, and his or her reason for applying.

Fill in your **personal information** so that the employer can contact you.

Indicate the position you are applying for in the **employment desired** section.

In the **work experience** part of the application, write something you've done, such as dog walking or babysitting. This section also shows where you have previously worked.

APPLICATION FOR EMPLOYMENT

Your Personal Information

Name: ____

             (Last)   *(First)*   *(Middle)*

Address: ____

____

    E-mail Address   *Telephone*

Employment Desired ___________________________

Date You Can Start: _________________________

Salary Wanted: ______________________________

Position: ____________________________________

Education: ___________________________________

____

Work Experience

____

Name and Address of Company

____

Date Started   *Date Left Position*

____

Supervisor

Why would you make a good worker?
Write two reasons below.

1. ____

2. ____

Sign Your Name ______________________________

Resume

A **resume** is a brief summary of relevant and important information about yourself that you would want to give to a possible employer. A resume is updated and changed each time you have new employment, educational or personal information you want to add.

The **personal information** section needs to be current so an employer can contact you.

The **education** section gives the employer an idea of what you have accomplished and what interests you might have.

The **work experience** section lists previous work experience you have had.

The **reference** section gives the names of a few people who the employer may contact to ask about you as a person or as a worker.

RESUME

Kevin Safford
44 Fern Street
Austin, TX 78705
397-987-0965
ksafford@tam.edu

Employment Desired
Playground Monitor

Education

| 2007–present | Austin High School, Austin, Texas |
| 2004–2007 | Austin Middle School, Austin, Texas |

Work Experience

2005–present **Paper Carrier**
Six days a week. Deliver newspapers.

2006–2007 **Volunteer,** *Austin Animal Shelter*
Two afternoons a week. Assist veterinary technicians.

References

Christopher Keefe, Manager of Delivery, Austin Daily News
397-898-0065

Rolando Torres, Director, Austin Animal Shelter
397-976-4593

Talk About It Discuss the questions with a partner or in a small group. If you were to apply for employment, what kinds of information would you include on your resume? What kind of work experience do you have? Complete the sentence frame. Then, write your own resume, using the model above as an example.

I would include these details on my resume: _______________________

____

____

____.

Business Letter

A **business letter** is a formal exchange in writing between two people. It is about professional or commercial interests. One format for a business letter is called a *block style.* This is where the return address, date, closing, signature, and typed name begin at the left side of the page.

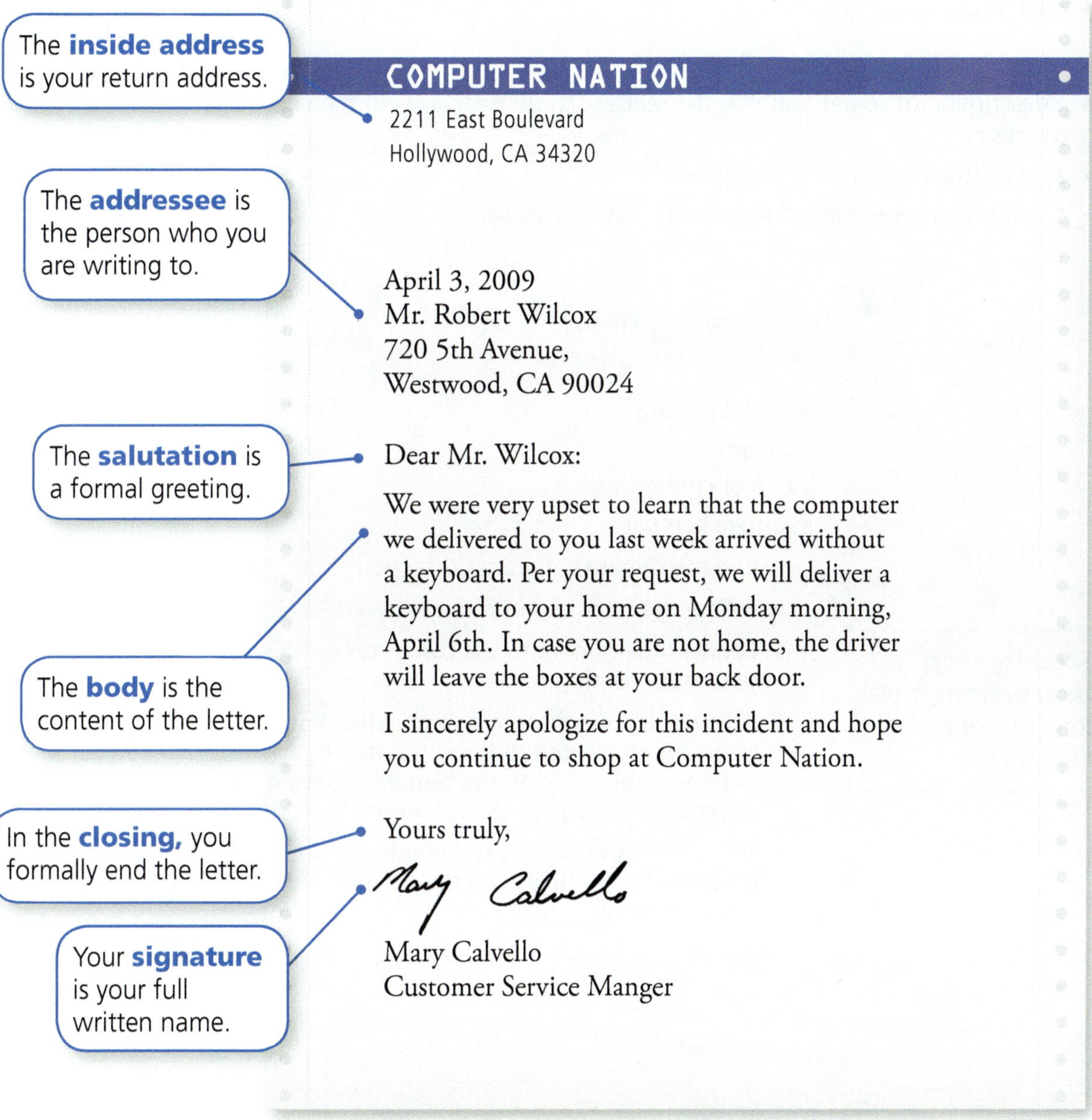

Talk About It Read the letter with a partner. Discuss the structure and sections of the letter. Have you ever written a formal letter? Why? If you haven't, discuss who you might write to and why.

Instruction Manual

An **instruction manual** gives step-by-step directions for finishing a task. The instructions can explain a number of items, such as:

- how to put something together
- how to do something
- how to use something

Most instructional manuals have these features:

- a description of something that the reader can do by following the directions
- a list of the materials the reader needs
- a series of steps explained in an order that makes sense

8

Transferring Digital Images to Your Computer

- digital camera
- computer
- USB or connecting cord
- camera software

1. Run the camera software CD on your computer.

2. Follow the steps to setup the software.

3. Connect the camera to the computer using the USB or connecting cord.

4. Follow the prompts that pop up when your camera is connected to the computer. If nothing pops up, open the camera program by selecting it from your "Start" menu.

5. Select "Transfer Images to Computer" or other similar feature from the camera software menu.

Step-by-step instructions explain the order of how to do something.

English-Spanish Glossary

How to Use This Glossary

This glossary can help you understand some of the words in this book. The entries in this glossary are in English alphabetical order. There are also guide words at the top of each page to show you the first and last words on the page. A Spanish definition appears with each English word. Each word also contains an abbreviation that tells you the part of speech. Here are the meanings for each abbreviation:

adj. = adjective   *n.* = noun
adv. = adverb   *v.* = verb

Remember, if you can't find the word you are looking for, ask for help or check a dictionary.

Cómo usar este glosario

Este glosario te puede servir para entender algunas palabras del libro. Las entradas de este glosario están en orden alfabético según el inglés. También hay palabras guía al principio de cada página para que sepas cuál es la primera y la última palabra de la página. Cada palabra aparece con una definición. También hay una abreviatura que indica de qué parte de la oración se trata. Estos son los significados de las abreviaturas:

adj. = adjetivo   *sust.* = sustantivo
adv. = adverbio   *v.* = verbo

Recuerda que si no encuentras la palabra que buscas, pide ayuda o consulta un diccionario.

Aa

abbreviation: *n.* a shortened form of a word or phrase, such as Dr. for Doctor or Rd. for Road *(cognate: abreviatura)*
abreviatura: *sust.* una palabra escrita de forma corta eliminando algunas letras. Ej. Dr. por Doctor o Sr. por Señor

adapt: *v.* to change in order to fit a new situation *(cognate: adaptar)*
adaptar: *v.* modificar algo para que se ajuste a una nueva situación

adjust: *v.* to make changes as you do something *(cognate: ajustar)*
ajustar: *v.* hacer cambios a algo para que funcione bien

adversity: *n.* troubles caused by bad luck *(cognate: adversidad)*
adversidad: *sust.* problemas causados por situaciones desfavorables

advertising: *n.* the display of products on the radio, on television, or in stores, which makes people want to buy them
publicidad: *sust.* promocionar un producto o servicio a través de un medio de comunicación o en las mismas tiendas, para que la gente lo compre

alike: *adj.* the same
parecido: *adj.* iguales

analyze: *v.* to examine or to look at very closely *(cognate: analizar)*
analizar: *v.* examinar algo cuidadosamente

anticipate: *v.* to look forward to, expect, or make plans for something
anticipar: *v.* pensar que algo va a suceder o podría suceder; predecir algo

approach: *n.* an organized way to do something or to get somewhere
enfoque: *sust.* una forma particular de abordar o analizar algo, o de emprender una acción

appropriate: *adj.* right or fitting for a situation *(cognate: apropiado)*
apropiado: *adj.* que es correcto; que encaja o corresponde a una situación

argument: *n.* a reason that is given to support or oppose a point of view *(cognate: argumento)*
argumento: *sust.* razonamiento que se emplea para probar o negar una proposición

artificial intelligence: *n.* a type of science that tries to simulate human intelligence *(cognate: inteligencia artificial)*
inteligencia artificial: *sust.* una rama de la ciencia que usa la tecnología para imitar la inteligencia humana

attributes: *n.* the qualities or characteristics of a particular person, place, or thing *(cognate: atributos)*
atributos: *sust.* características; cualidades

awareness: *n.* knowledge that something exists
conciencia: *sust.* conocimiento de que algo existe

Bb

background: *n.* a person's experience or knowledge; the culture and values with which a person has been raised
formación: *sust.* experiencia y conocimientos de una persona; la cultura y los valores con los que ha sido criada

besieged: *v.* to be surrounded by negative forces
asediado: *adj.* estar acosado o abrumado por pensamientos negativos

English-Spanish Glossary

bias: *n.* an opinion that affects the way you present information
parcialidad: *sust.* opinión predispuesta o prejuiciosa, que afecta la forma en que se presenta la información

billboard: *n.* a large outdoor sign
cartelera: *sust.* un cartel grande que sirve para anunciar algo, casi siempre al aire libre

bravery: *n.* the quality of having courage or being fearless
valentía: *sust.* valor; la calidad de tener coraje o no tener miedo

breakthrough: *n.* an important discovery or invention
avance: *sust.* un importante descubrimiento o invención

Cc

cause: *n.* why something happens; a reason (cognate: causa)
causa: *sust.* motivo por el que sucede algo

change: *n.* the act of making something different from what it was
cambio: *sust.* cuando algo deja de ser como era antes; modificación

character: *n.* what makes you the type of person you are (cognate: carácter)
carácter: *sust.* conjunto de cualidades propios de una persona

characteristic: *n.* something that is unique to a specific thing or person (cognate: característica)
característica: *sust.* cualidad o particularidad que describe a una persona o cosa

clarify: *v.* to make clear
aclarar: *v.* explicar algo que no está claro

clique: *n.* an exclusive group of people that may keep other people out of its group
grupo cerrado: *sust.* un grupo de personas, del cual es muy difícil formar parte

collision: *n.* a violent crash or accident (cognate: colisión)
colisión: *sust.* choque violento o accidente

compare: *v.* to show how things are alike or similar (cognate: comparar)
comparar: *v.* mostrar en que se parecen dos o más cosas

comprehend: *v.* to understand something (cognate: comprender)
comprender: *v.* entender algo

compromise: *n.* an agreement in which neither side gets everything it wanted
acuerdo: *sust.* resultado positivo de una negociación entre dos o más personas, en el que ambas partes ceden en algo

conceive: *v.* to think or imagine something (cognate: concebir)
concebir: *v.* crear; imaginar algo

concerns: *n.* worries or fears
preocupación: *sust.* asunto inquietante; problema

concession: *n.* something you give up, often when you don't want to (cognate: concesión)
concesión: *sust.* acción de ceder, regalar o dar algo como favor o excepción

conclude: *v.* to use clues to figure out something not stated; to form an opinion based on evidence (cognate: concluir)
concluir: *v.* usar claves para resolver algo que no está dicho expresamente; formarse una opinión basándose en la evidencia

concrete: *adj.* real or exact (cognate: concreto)
concreto: *adj.* algo en particular; preciso; que se puede tocar

conduct: *v.* to carry out or manage an activity (cognate: conducir)
conducir: *v.* llevar a cabo o dirigir una actividad

confirm: *v.* to check to make sure something is true (cognate: confirmar)
confirmar: *v.* revisar o comprobar, para asegurarse de que algo es cierto

confrontation: *n.* a dispute, fight, or argument (cognate: confrontación)
confrontación: *sust.* enfrentamiento, disputa, discusión

confusion: *n.* the act of being mixed up, unclear, or unsure about something (cognate: confusión)
confusión: *sust.* lío; mala interpretación; que no se ha entendido claramente

connect: *v.* to show how things are related (cognate: conectar)
conectar: *v.* mostrar cómo se relacionan las cosas

connection: *n.* the state of two things fitting together; when people or groups relate on an emotional level (cognate: conexión)
conexión: *sust.* unión o enlace entre dos cosas; entenderse a nivel afectivo

consider: *v.* to think carefully about something (cognate: considerar)
considerar: *v.* tomar en cuenta algo

constant: *adj.* staying the same, happening over and over, or always there (cognate: constante)
constante: *adj.* que no cambia; que se repite; continuo

consult: *v.* to look for information from resources or people (cognate: consultar)
consultar: *v.* buscar información en fuentes o preguntar a otras personas

context: *n.* surrounding text or information (cognate: contexto)
contexto: *sust.* información o texto en el entorno

continuum: *n.* a series of things that become different gradually (cognate: continuo)
continuo: *sust.* una serie de cosas que cambian con el tiempo

contrast: *v.* to show how things are different (cognate: contrastar)
contrastar: *v.* mostrar en qué se diferencian las cosas

convey: *v.* to communicate something in words, pictures or other ways
transmitir: *v.* expresar algo con palabras, imágenes u otros medios

courage: *n.* the mental strength to face a difficult or dangerous situation (cognate: coraje)
coraje: *sust.* fuerza mental para enfrentarse a situaciones difíciles o peligrosas

cultural: *adj.* something related to everyday life that is shared by people in a given place or time (cognate: cultural)
cultural: *adj.* relacionado con el conjunto de costumbres y modos de vida de un grupo social o una época

Dd

debate: *n.* a discussion of arguments in favor of and against a certain action (cognate: *debate*)
debate: *sust.* presentación de razonamientos a favor y en contra de una acción específica

demonstration: *n.* a public display of a group's feelings (cognate: *demostración*)
demostración: *sust.* manifestación pública que hace un grupo de personas para demostrar su opinión

detail: *n.* a piece of information (cognate: *detalle*)
detalle: *sust.* un pedazo específico de información

determination: *n.* the strong desire and drive to reach a goal (cognate: *determinación*)
determinación: *sust.* resolución; estar decidido a alcanzar un objetivo

development: *n.* when something gets bigger, fuller, or better
desarrollo: *sust.* crecimiento, mejora, ampliación o progreso

devise: *v.* to make something and to figure out how it will work
idear: *v.* inventar o planificar algo

different: *adj.* not the same (cognate: *diferente*)
diferente: *adj.* que no es igual

differentiate: *v.* to notice or show the difference between two things (cognate: *diferenciar*)
diferenciar: *v.* mostrar las características que distinguen a una persona o cosa de otra

dilemma: *n.* a very difficult and unpleasant choice (cognate: *dilema*)
dilema: *sust.* conflicto que requiere escoger una de dos opciones

discern: *v.* to become aware of something that is hard to understand or see (cognate: *discernir*)
discernir: *v.* darse cuenta de algo que es difícil de deducir o entender

discipline: *n.* the ability to control your thoughts or behavior (cognate: *disciplina*)
disciplina: *sust.* la habilidad de controlar los impulsos, comportamientos y pensamientos; fuerza de voluntad para cumplir con los deberes u obligaciones

discourse: *n.* a serious conversation about something (cognate: *discurso*)
discurso: *sust.* conversación o reflexión sobre un tema serio

discrimination: *n.* treating people unfairly because they belong to a particular group (cognate: *discriminación*)
discriminación: *s.* trato injusto a las personas porque pertenecen a cierto grupo

discuss: *v.* to talk about a subject
discutir o tratar: *v.* hablar sobre un tema con otras personas

disgusting: *adj.* very offensive or insulting
repugnante: *adj.* muy desagradable, asqueroso, insultante

distinguish: *v.* to tell the difference between similar things (cognate: *distinguir*)
distinguir: *v.* diferenciar por alguna particularidad

distortion: *n.* the act of changing the truth to give people a false idea
distorsión: *sust.* cambio del sentido o aspecto original; deformación

distracting: *adj.* disturbing or causing worry or alarm (cognate: *distracción*)
distracción: *sust.* olvido; descuido que puede causar preocupación o alarma

dress code: *n.* a set of rules that say what people can wear in a specific place, like a school
etiqueta en el vestir: *sust.* normas que rigen la manera de vestir en un determinado lugar, como la escuela

Ee

effect: *n.* what happens next after something occurs; the result (cognate: *efecto*)
efecto: *sust.* lo que sucede como consecuencia de una acción; el resultado

element: *n.* a part or piece of; another word for detail (cognate: *elemento*)
elemento: *sust.* pieza o componente; una parte integrante de algo

emotion: *n.* a feeling, such as happiness, anger, or sadness (cognate: *emoción*)
emoción: *sust.* cambio intenso en el ánimo, por ejemplo, tristeza, alegría o rabia

empathy: *n.* understanding and sharing another person's feelings (cognate: *empatía*)
empatía: *sust.* capacidad de entender y compartir los sentimientos de otra persona

endangered: *n.* in danger of becoming extinct
en vías de extinción: *sust.* en peligro de desaparecer

enlighten: *v.* to give people information that helps them understand
iluminar: *v.* enseñar; aclarar algo

evaluate: *v.* to make a judgment about a person, place, or thing based on what you know (cognate: *evaluar*)
evaluar: *v.* formarse una opinión acerca de una persona, lugar o cosa con la información disponible

evidence: *n.* detail that shows that something is true (cognate: *evidencia*)
evidencia: *sust.* detalle que demuestra que algo es verdad

evolve: *v.* to slowly improve over time (cognate: *evolucionar*)
evolucionar: *v.* progresar lentamente

expectations: *n.* what you think or hope will happen in the future (cognate: *expectativas*)
expectativas: *sust.* lo que se piensa o espera que suceda en el futuro

explanation: *n.* a statement that helps you understand a situation or an idea (cognate: *explicación*)
explicación: *sust.* enunciado que ayuda a otros a entender una idea o situación

extreme: *adj.* much more than ordinary, usual or expected (cognate: *extremo*)
extremo: *adj.* excesivo; mucho más que lo ordinario, común o anticipado

Ff

fact: *n.* a statement that can be proven true
hecho: *sust.* un enunciado que es cierto y comprobable

fame: *n.* the state of being widely honored and praised (cognate: *fama*)
fama: *sust.* reconocimiento; ser conocido y alabado

former: *adj.* when something already happened or existed in the past
previo: *adj.* algo que ya sucedió o existió con anterioridad

formulate: *v.* to create or to prepare (cognate: *formular*)
formular: *v.* crear o proponer

free speech: *n.* a natural right for U.S. citizens to speak, without restrictions or limits
libre expresión: *sust.* el derecho de expresar las ideas libremente, sin restricciones ni límites, que tienen los ciudadanos de los Estados Unidos

freedom: *n.* the power to act, speak, or think as one chooses
libertad: *sust.* el poder de hablar o actuar según los deseos de cada uno

frequently: *adv.* happening often (cognate: *frecuentemente*)
frecuentemente: *adv.* que sucede a menudo

Gg

greed: *n.* an intense desire to have a lot of money or own a lot of things
codicia: *sust.* deseo excesivo de riquezas y bienes materiales

growth: *n.* the act of developing or becoming larger
crecimiento: *sust.* aumento de tamaño; desarrollo

Hh

happiness: *n.* to be happy
felicidad: *sust.* ser feliz

harmful: *adj.* capable of causing much damage
pernicioso: *adj.* perjudicial; que puede causar daño

heroism: *n.* the qualities of being a hero (cognate: *heroísmo*)
heroísmo: *sust.* la cualidad de realizar grandes hazañas

historical: *adj.* having to do with history (cognate: *histórico*)
histórico: *adj.* perteneciente o relativo a la historia

history: *n.* an account of things that have happened in the past (cognate: *historia*)
historia: *sust.* recuento de los hechos que han sucedido en el pasado

honor: *v.* to do what you have agreed to
cumplir: *v.* hacer aquello que se ha acordado

horror: *n.* a very deep fear (cognate: *horror*)
horror: *sust.* un miedo intenso y profundo

humiliate: *v.* to make fun of someone (cognate: *humillar*)
humillar: *v.* burlarse de alguien

Ii

identity: *n.* the set of characteristics that make you who you are (cognate: *identidad*)
identidad: *sust.* conjunto de rasgos particulares que te definen como persona

ignorance: *n.* lack of knowledge about something (cognate: *ignorancia*)
ignorancia: *sust.* falta de conocimiento sobre las cosas

illustrate: *v.* to provide pictures of an idea or to give examples of it (cognate: *ilustrar*)
ilustrar: *v.* explicar con imágenes una idea; dar ejemplo

immigrant: *n.* a person who comes to a new country in order to live there (cognate: *inmigrante*)
inmigrante: *sust.* persona que llega a un país nuevo con el propósito de establecerse ahí

implied: *adj.* not expressed directly
insinuado: *adj.* dado a entender de modo indirecto

important detail: *n.* a key piece of information (cognate: *detalle importante*)
detalle importante: *sust.* una pieza de información clave

impression: *n.* a quick, general idea of someone or something (cognate: *impresión*)
impresión: *sust.* una opinión general sobre algo o alguien

improbable: *adj.* when something can happen but is not likely to (cognate: *improbable*)
improbable: *adj.* que no es muy probable que suceda

individual: *n.* one person (cognate: *individuo*)
individuo: *sust.* una persona

infer: assume something based on facts (cognate: *inferir*)
inferir: *v.* suponer algo basándose en hechos

influence: *n.* the effect of something on a person, a thing, or an event (cognate: *influencia*)
influencia: *sust.* efecto de algo sobre una persona, cosa o evento

inherent: *adj.* relating to the basic nature of a person or thing (cognate: *inherente*)
inherente: *adj.* que es propio o forma parte de algo o alguien

insight: *n.* a clear understanding
perspicacia: *sust.* la habilidad de percibir o entender algo claramente

instinct: *n.* a natural reaction to something (cognate: *instinto*)
instinto: *sust.* reacción natural a una situación

integrity: *n.* high moral standards; honesty (cognate: *integridad*)
integridad: *sust.* honradez, fidelidad a los propios valores o creencias

intent: *n.* a purpose
intención: *sust.* determinación para alcanzar un fin

interact: *v.* to talk, behave, or have some kind of exchange with people
interaccionar: *v.* hablar, comunicar o tener algún intercambio con otras personas

interpretation: *n.* the meaning you find in events, pictures, or words (cognate: *interpretación*)
interpretación: *sust.* significado que se le da a una palabra, imagen o hecho

intuition: *n.* a very quick and strong insight (cognate: *intuición*)
intuición: *sust.* comprensión instantánea de las cosas sin necesidad de razonamiento

involve: *v.* to include or be part of something (cognate: *involucrar*)
involucrar: *v.* incluir; formar parte de algo

irony: *n.* the difference between what is expected to happen and what actually happens *(cognate: ironía)*
ironía: *sust.* incongruencia entre lo que se esperaba y lo que en realidad ocurrió

isolation: *n.* the act of being set apart from other people or a feeling of loneliness
aislamiento: *sust.* separación; sensación de estar alejado o apartado de otras personas

Kk

knowledge: *n.* information gained when you understand certain facts, situations, or ideas; information acquired from study or through experience
conocimiento: *sust.* saber obtenido al entender conceptos, hechos, ideas o situaciones; información adquirida a través del estudio o la experiencia

Ll

language: *n.* the set of words a group of people uses to communicate with each other
idioma: *sust.* las palabras que un grupo de personas utiliza para comunicarse entre sí

legendary: *adj.* being famous because of a special talent or skill *(cognate: legendario)*
legendario: *adj.* que es conocido o famoso por sus hazañas o talentos

logical: *adj.* makes sense *(cognate: lógico)*
lógico: *adj.* que tiene sentido o es razonable

luck: *n.* something that brings good or bad things to someone
suerte: *sust.* azar; cosas buenas o malas que le suceden a una persona

Mm

main idea: *n.* the topic
idea principal: *sust.* el tema

manipulate: *v.* to manage or control people unfairly *(cognate: manipular)*
manipular: *v.* controlar de manera artera a las personas

materialistic: *adj.* when you want to buy and own things *(cognate: materialista)*
materialista: *adj.* dícese de una persona que desea adquirir o poseer bienes

meaning: *n.* the purpose or intention of something
significado: *sust.* propósito o intención

mechanism: *n.* a process, technique or system that helps you achieve something *(cognate: mecanismo)*
mecanismo: *sust.* proceso, técnica, sistema o estructura que permite lograr algo

media: *n.* the various formats of mass communication, such as TV, radio, the Internet, and newspapers
medios de comunicación: *sust.* instrumentos a través de los cuales se comunica de forma masiva, tales como: TV, radio, Internet y periódicos

misinterpret: *v.* to be incorrect about the meaning of words or gestures *(cognate: malinterpretar)*
malinterpretar: *v.* no interpretar correctamente palabras o gestos

modified: *adj.* when something has had small changes made to it *(cognate: modificado)*
modificado: *adj.* que ha sido cambiado ligeramente

monarch: *n.* another word for a king, queen, or royal leader *(cognate: monarca)*
monarca: *sust.* rey, reina o dirigente de sangre real

motive: *n.* a person's reason for doing something *(cognate: motivo)*
motivo: *sust.* la razón por la que alguien hace algo

Nn

negotiate: *v.* to agree through discussion and compromise *(cognate: negociar)*
negociar: *v.* llegar a un acuerdo por medio del convenio

Oo

objective: *adj.* based on facts rather than on opinions or feelings *(cognate: objetivo)*
objetivo: *adj.* que está basado en hechos y no en opiniones o sentimientos

obligation: *n.* a duty; something you need to do *(cognate: obligación)*
obligación: *sust.* deber; conducta que resulta como parte de las normas o de lo que se espera

observe: *v.* to look at something closely or to study it *(cognate: observar)*
observar: *v.* mirar algo con detenimiento, con cuidado

opinion: *n.* expresses a belief or a viewpoint that should be supported by facts or reason *(cognate: opinión)*
opinión: *sust.* juicio o punto de vista que se apoya en hechos o en el entendimiento

opportunity: *n.* a good chance to advance or progress *(cognate: oportunidad)*
oportunidad: *sust.* ocasión; momento favorable para alcanzar algo o progresar

oppose: *v.* to resist or take a stand against a person or thing *(cognate: oponerse)*
oponerse: *v.* resistirse, tomar una postura frente a algo o alguien

oral history: *n.* a history that is collected and recorded through an interview
historia oral: *sust.* historia que se recoge y se registra por medio de una entrevista

overemphasis: *n.* too much importance on one thing
enfatizar: *sust.* el hecho de darle mucha importancia a algo

Pp

paraphrase: *v.* to restate in your own words *(cognate: parafrasear)*
parafrasear: *v.* explicar algo en tus propias palabras

pattern: *n.* a routine or set way of doing something *(cognate: patrón)*
patrón: *sust.* pauta; modelo; una conducta que se repite

pause: *v.* to stop reading aloud *(cognate: pausa)*
pausa: *v.* detener brevemente la lectura en voz alta

perception: *n.* what you see or understand about things that happen around you *(cognate: percepción)*
percepción: *sust.* la impresión que se tiene sobre hechos que suceden en el entorno

persevere: *v.* to continue to do something or believe something, even when it is difficult to do so (cognate: perseverar)
perseverar: *v.* continuar haciendo o creyendo algo hasta alcanzar el objetivo, aunque resulte muy difícil

perspective: *n.* your point of view, or the way you see and understand something (cognate: perspectiva)
perspectiva: *sust.* punto de vista personal; la manera de ver y entender algo

persuasive appeals: *n.* the arguments an author makes
argumentos convincentes: *sust.* razones que da una persona a otra para convencerla

persuasive techniques: *n.* devices used to influence the audience in favor of the author's argument
técnicas persuasivas: *sust.* métodos usados por una persona o grupo para convencer a un público de que realice una acción a su favor

positive: *adj.* describes something that is good (cognate: positivo)
positivo: *adj.* que es bueno o favorable

possible: *adj.* can be done or can happen (cognate: posible)
posible: *adj.* que se puede hacer o que puede suceder

predict: *v.* to figure out what might happen next (cognate: predecir)
predecir: *v.* adivinar o suponer lo que puede suceder en el futuro

presume: *v.* to believe something is true without getting proof (cognate: presumir)
presumir: *v.* creer algo sin verificarlo o sin tener pruebas

prevent: *v.* to keep something from happening
prevenir: *v.* hacer algo para que evitar que suceda un hecho

principles: *n.* important basic truths or rules of behavior (cognate: principios)
principios: *sust.* norma personal que rige las conductas

process: *n.* a series of steps taken to do a task or meet a goal (cognate: proceso)
proceso: *sust.* forma de hacer algo de manera ordenada y metódica para lograr una meta

produce: *v.* to make something (cognate: producir)
producir: *v.* elaborar algo

progress: *n.* movement toward a goal (cognate: progreso)
progreso: *sust.* avance, mejora o adelanto

protect: *v.* to shield someone or something from danger or injury (cognate: proteger)
proteger: *v.* cuidar; defender a alguien o algo de un peligro o un posible daño

protest: *n.* the act of disagreeing against something (cognate: protesta)
protestar: *v.* expresar el desacuerdo sobre algo

psychology: *n.* the science of how human beings feel and behave (cognate: psicología)
psicología: *sust.* ciencia que estudia el comportamiento y la manera de sentir de las personas

punctuation: *n.* the marks you see in sentences, like a period or a comma (cognate: puntuación)
puntuación: *sust.* signos que se usan en las oraciones, como el punto o la coma

Qq

question: *n.* a sentence that looks for an answer; v. to challenge the truth of something (cognate: cuestionar)
cuestión o pregunta: *sust.* enunciado que busca una respuesta ; cuestionar: v. controvertir una verdad dudosa

Rr

radical: *adj.* extreme or very different from the usual (cognate: radical)
radical: *adj.* extremo o muy alejado de lo promedio o lo usual

reaction: *n.* a particular behavior in response to something (cognate: reacción)
reacción: *sust.* algo que sucede como respuesta a otra cosa o estímulo

read fluently: *v.* to read smoothly while also understanding the text and what the author is saying
leer con fluidez: *v.* leer sin saltos ni pausas, entendiendo el texto y lo que el autor quiere decir

reading rate: *n.* your reading speed
índice de velocidad de lectura: *sust.* velocidad a la que una persona lee

reality: *n.* real things, facts, or events (cognate: realidad)
realidad: *sust.* todo lo que constituye el mundo real: objetos, hechos o eventos,

reconciliation: *n.* the act of ending a disagreement and becoming friendly again (cognate: reconciliación)
reconciliación: *sust.* hacer las paces después de una pelea o disgusto

reflect: *v.* to think calmly and carefully; to give something serious thought (cognate: reflexionar)
reflexionar: *v.* considerar algo con detenimiento; pensar seriamente sobre un tema

relationship: *n.* when two people feel connected to each other (cognate: relación)
relación: *sust.* la conexión entre dos cosas o personas

represent: *v.* to act out the example of something (cognate: representar)
representar: *v.* actuar; imitar

resolute: *adj.* setting a goal and sticking to it (cognate: resuelto)
resuelto: *adj.* tener determinación para alcanzar un objetivo

resolve: *v.* to deal with a problem successfully by fixing it (cognate: resolver)
resolver: *v.* solucionar un problema de manera satisfactoria

respond: *v.* to react to someone or something by thinking, speaking, or taking action (cognate: responder)
responder: *v.* contestar; tomar acción como respuesta a la acción de otra persona

responsibility: *n.* something that you really have to do; your job (cognate: responsabilidad)
responsabilidad: *sust.* trabajo o tarea que te toca hacer; deber u obligación

restate: *v.* to say in another way
reformular: *v.* volver a plantear algo diciéndolo de otra manera

results: *n.* outcomes or effects (cognate: resultados)
resultados: *sust.* efectos, consecuencias

revise: *v.* to make corrections to something in order to improve it; to look again and correct (*cognate: revisar*)
revisar: *v.* mirar otra vez, examinar y corregir algo para mejorarlo

rivalry: *n.* a strong or intense competition (*cognate: rivalidad*)
rivalidad: *sust.* oposición intensa entre dos partes; competencia

royalty: *n.* having to do with nobility, such as kings and queens (*cognate: realeza*)
realeza: *sust.* de origen noble, por ejemplo un rey o reina

Ss

sacrifice: *v.* to give up something in order to help someone else or get something else (*cognate: sacrificar*)
sacrificar: *v.* renunciar a algo para ayudar alguien más o para conseguir algo

salary: *n.* the money you make for a job (*cognate: salario*)
salario: *sust.* sueldo; el dinero que gana un empleado

scandal: *n.* an outrage or a disgraceful event (*cognate: escándalo*)
escándalo: *sust.* situación o hecho que causa indignación o revuelo

science fiction: *n.* a type of fiction that uses science concepts to tell stories (*cognate: ciencia ficción*)
ciencia ficción: *sust.* tipo de relatos de ficción que transcurren en medio de grandes avances científicos imaginarios

self-expression: *n.* the act of communicating to others your own feelings and personality
autoexpresión: *sust.* el acto de comunicar a otros los propios sentimientos, ideas y personalidad

selflessness: *n.* the act of putting the needs or wishes of other people ahead of your own
altruísmo: *sust.* las necesidades o deseos de los demás por delante de las de uno mismo

shudder: *v.* to shake or shiver
estremecerse: *v.* temblar, sacudirse por un escalofrío

sibling: *n.* a brother or sister
hermano o hermana: *sust.*

similar: *adj.* the same (*cognate: similar*)
similar: *adj.* parecido

smokejumper: *n.* a special kind of firefighter who fights forest fires
bombero paracaidista: *sust.* bomberos forestales que saltan desde avionetas en paracaídas para apagar fuegos en terrenos remotos o bosques de difícil acceso

special effects: *n.* sounds and other features that are used in movies (*cognate: efectos especiales*)
efectos especiales: *sust.* sonidos e imágenes fabricados artificialmente para dar una impresión de realismo en las películas.

sprawl: *v.* to spread out without any control
extender sin control: *v.* expandir o propagarse rápidamente

squelch: *v.* to not allow something to happen
suprimir: *v.* impedir que alguien haga algo o que algo suceda

stated: *adj.* expressed directly
indicado: *adj.* expresado directamente

statement: *n.* an expression of an idea or opinion
declaración: *sust.* expresión de ideas, opiniones o sentimientos

statistics: *n.* facts presented in number form (*cognate: estadística*)
estadística: *sust.* hechos que se presentan de forma numérica

stereotype: *n.* a belief about a group of people, based on knowing only a few (*cognate: estereotipo*)
estereotipo: *sust.* la imagen o idea que se tiene sobre un grupo de personas, basándose sólo en las características resaltantes de algunos de sus miembros

struggle: *v.* to keep on doing something even though it is difficult to do
luchar: *v.* pelear; abrirse paso; seguir adelante a pesar de las dificultades

subjective: *adj.* based on feelings or opinions rather than facts (*cognate: sujetivo*)
subjetivo: *adj.* que está basado en opiniones o sentimientos y no en datos o hechos

summarize: *v.* to briefly state the most important events or ideas in a story or article
resumir: *v.* decir de forma breve las ideas o puntos principales

superhero: *n.* a fictional heroic character (*cognate: superhéroe*)
superhéroe: *s.* personaje de la ficción que tiene poderes especiales y es un héroe

superiority: *n.* the quality of feeling better or more important than others (*cognate: superioridad*)
superioridad: *sust.* la cualidad de sentirse mejor o más importante que los demás

superpowers: *n.* very strong powers
super poderes: *sust.* poderes especiales, extraordinarios

support: *v.* to provide evidence for something
respaldar: *v.* suministrar evidencia de algo

supporting detail: *n.* information that helps you understand the main idea or topic
detalle de respaldo: *s.* información que ayuda a entender la idea principal o el tema

Tt

text message: *n.* a communication you send with a cell phone
mensaje de texto (SMS): *sust.* comunicación escrita enviada por un teléfono celular

theft: *n.* stealing something from someone
robo: *sust.* apropiarse de algo que pertenece a otra persona

tradition: *n.* an important belief or custom passed down through time (*cognate: tradición*)
tradición: *sust.* creencia o costumbre pasada de generación a generación

Uu

uncertainty: *n.* doubt, lack of belief (*cognate: incertidumbre*)
incertidumbre: *sust.* duda o la creencia en algo

understanding: *n.* a knowledge of what something means
comprensión: *sust.* conocimiento del significado de algo

unify: *v.* to bring people or things together *(cognate: unificar)*
unificar: *v.* unir, hacer de muchas cosas separadas un todo

universal: *adj.* involving everyone in the world or in a specific group *(cognate: universal)*
universal: *adj.* que pertenece o es válido para todo el mundo

unlucky: *adj.* to have bad luck
desafortunado: *adj.* sin suerte; lamentable

Vv

verbal: *adj.* made up of words *(cognate: verbal)*
verbal: *adj.* dicho con palabras; oral

verify: *v.* to check whether or not something is true *(cognate: verificar)*
verificar: *v.* revisar; comprobar si algo es cierto

visualize: *v.* to create a mental picture *(cognate: visualizar)*
visualizar: *v.* hacerse una imagen mental

Ww

wage gap: *n.* the difference between men's pay and women's pay
brecha salarial: *sust.* las diferencias de salario entre personas de diferentes grupos, por ejemplo entre los hombres y las mujeres

warning: *n.* a message informing of danger
advertencia: *s.* un mensaje o señal que indica peligro

wildfire: *n.* an unplanned fire that causes damage to forests and other wild areas
incendio forestal: *s.* un incendio que empieza por accidente y que causa gran daño a un bosques o zona silvestre

winnings: *n.* something won, especially money
ganancias: *sust.* dinero ganado, beneficios

witness: *n.* someone who sees something and reports it
testigo: *sust.* alguien que presencia un hecho

worldview: *n.* the values and beliefs held by a culture
visión del mundo: *sust.* los valores y creencias de una cultura

Index

I2

Writing

Extension Activities

Credits

Illustration

Background images on Reading pages by Robin Storesund

Photographs

Every effort has been made to secure permission and provide appropriate credit for photographic material. The publisher deeply regrets any omission and pledges to correct errors called to its attention in subsequent editions.

Unless otherwise acknowledged, all photographs are the property of Pearson Education, Inc.

Photo locators denoted as follows: Top (T), Center (C), Bottom (B), Left (L), Right (R), Background (Bkgd)

Cover and Title Page: *Girl* ©Jean Maurice/Getty Images; *camel* Getty Images; *pyramid* ©Sylvain Grandadam; *elevator* Getty Images, Inc. Digital Vision; **iii** (CL) ©Brand X/SuperStock, (TL) ©Chris Sattlberger/Corbis, (T) ©Mike Danton /Alamy Images, (B) David Peart/©DK Images, (BL) Zena Holloway/Getty Images; **iv** (BL) ©indykb/Alamy, (CL) ©Photodisc/SuperStock, (T) ©RubberBall/SuperStock, (TL) David McGlynn/Getty Images; **v** (TL) ©Image Source, (CL) ©moodboard/SuperStock, (T) Brendan Tobin/Getty Images; **vi** (BL) ©Image Source, (TL) ©Robert Landau/Corbis, (CL) AP Images, (T) UNIVERSAL/The Kobal Collection; **vii** (BL) ©Hulton-Deutsch Collection/Corbis, (TL) ©Stephen Bisgrove/Alamy, (T, CL) Getty Images; viii (T) ©George Steinmetz/Corbis, (BL) ©Kevin R. Morris/Corbis, (TL) ©L. Zacharie/Alamy Images, (CL) ©Pictorial Press Ltd/Alamy Images; **L1** (T) ©Design Pics Inc./Alamy, (B) ©Judith Collins/Alamy; **L3** ©Blend Images/Alamy; **1** (CR) ©Brand X/SuperStock, (TR) ©Chris Sattlberger/Corbis, (T) ©Mike Danton/Alamy Images, (B) Corbis, (BR) David Peart/©DK Images, (BC) Zena Holloway/Getty Images; **2** ©James O'Mara/Taxi/Getty Images, Inc.; **4** Steve Gorton/©DK Images; **5** Ron Chapple/Taxi/Getty Images; **6** ©Mike Danton/Alamy Images; **7** Stephen Stickler/Getty Images; **8** ©BananaStock/SuperStock; **10** (Bkgd) ©Chris Sattlberger/Corbis, (BR) Corbis; **11** Getty Images; **13** ©Blend Images/SuperStock; **14** ©Corbis/SuperStock; **15** ©Brand X/SuperStock; **18** (BR) David Peart/©DK Images, Zena Holloway/Getty Images; **19** National Geographic/Getty Images; **21** Digital Vision; **24** (CR) ©Brand X/SuperStock, (TR) ©Chris Sattlberger/Corbis, (T) ©Mike Danton/Alamy Images, (BR) David Peart/©DK Images, (BC) Zena Holloway/Getty Images; **25** (BC) ©indykb/Alamy, (CR) ©Photodisc/SuperStock, (T) ©RubberBall/SuperStock, (TR) David McGlynn/Getty Images, (B) Jupiter Images; **26** Flying Colours Ltd./Digital Vision/Getty Images, Inc; **28** David Young/PhotoEdit; **29** Dave King/©DK Images; **30** ©RubberBall/SuperStock; **31** ©Design Pics Inc./Alamy; **32** Getty Images; **34** David McGlynn/Getty Images; **35** ©Corbis/SuperStock; **37** Jupiter Images; **38** ©Blend Images/SuperStock; **39** ©Photodisc/SuperStock; **40** ©Comstock/SuperStock; **42** ©indykb/Alamy; **43** Jim Wark/Jupiter Images; **48** (B) ©indykb/Alamy, (CR) ©Photodisc/SuperStock, (T) ©RubberBall/SuperStock, (TR) David McGlynn/Getty Images; **49** (TR) ©Image Source, (CR) ©moodboard/SuperStock, (T) Brendan Tobin/Getty Images; **50** Getty Images, Inc.; **52** Brand X Pictures/Alamy Images; **54** Brendan Tobin/Getty Images; **55** John Atkinson Grimshaw/Getty Images; **58** ©Image Source; **59** ©Ian Shaw/Alamy; **62** Corbis/Jupiter Images; **63** ©moodboard/SuperStock; **65** Steve Gorton/DK Images; **66** Bettmann/Corbis; **67** ©Mark Harmel/Alamy Images; **72** (TR) ©Image Source, (CR) ©moodboard/SuperStock, (T) Brendan Tobin/Getty Images; **73** (BC) ©Image Source, (TR) ©Robert Landau/Corbis, (CR) AP Images, (T) UNIVERSAL/The Kobal Collection; **77** Steve Mason/Getty Images; **74** ©Neil Brennan/ Canopy Illustration/Veer; **78** ©Corbis/SuperStock; **79** UNIVERSAL/The Kobal Collection; **80** Getty Images; **82** ©Visions of America, LLC/Alamy; **83** ©Robert Landau/Corbis; **85** ©RubberBall/SuperStock; **86** AP Images; **87** George Disario/Corbis/Bettmann; **89** Tetra Images/Jupiter Images; **90** ©Brand X/SuperStock; **91** ©Image Source; **92** Radius Images/Jupiter Images; **96** (B) ©Image Source, (TR) ©Robert Landau/Corbis, (CR) AP Images, (T) UNIVERSAL/The Kobal Collection; **97** (BC) ©Hulton-Deutsch Collection/Corbis, (TR) ©Stephen Bisgrove/Alamy, (B) ©Visions of America, LLC/Alamy Images, (T, CR) Getty Images; **98** Ron Sanford/Corbis; **102** Getty Images; **103** ©Leif Skoogfors/Corbis; **106** ©Stephen Bisgrove/Alamy; **107** ©Reuters/Corbis; **109** John Stillwell/©AP Photo; **110** Penny Tweedie/Getty Images; **111** Getty Images; **113** ©Jonathan Nourok/PhotoEdit; **114** ©vario images GmbH & Co.KG/Alamy Images; **115** ©Hulton-Deutsch Collection/Corbis; **120** (B) ©Hulton-Deutsch Collection/Corbis, (TR) ©Stephen Bisgrove/Alamy, (T, CR) Getty Images; **121** (T) ©George Steinmetz/Corbis, (BC) ©Kevin R. Morris/Corbis, (TR) ©L. Zacharie/Alamy Images, (TR) ©Pictorial Press Ltd/Alamy Images, (B) ©Toshiyuki Aizawa/Corbis; **122** Masterfile; **126** ©William Whitehurst/Corbis; **127** ©George Steinmetz/Corbis; **129** ©Toshiyuki Aizawa/Corbis; **130** ©L. Zacharie/Alamy Images; **131** (TR, TL) Getty Images; **134** ©Pictorial Press Ltd/Alamy Images; **135** 20TH CENTURY FOX/The Kobal Collection; **138** ©Corbis/SuperStock; **139** ©Kevin R. Morris/Corbis; **144** (T) ©George Steinmetz/Corbis, (B) ©Kevin R. Morris/Corbis, (TR) ©L. Zacharie/Alamy Images, (CR) ©Pictorial Press Ltd/Alamy Images.